AFFINITY DIAGRAMS
STEP-BY-STEP GUIDE

2ND EDITION

Robert A Curedale
Copyright © 01 March 2019 by Robert A. Curedale
All rights reserved. Published by Design Community College Inc.

The publisher and author accept no liability, regardless of legal basis. Designations used in this book may be trademarks whose use by third parties for their own purposes could violate the rights of the owners. The author and publisher have taken great care with all texts and illustrations in this book. The information contained within this book is strictly for educational purposes. If you wish to apply ideas contained in this book you are taking full responsibility for your actions. There are no representations or warranties, express or implied, about the completeness, accuracy, reliability, suitability or availability with respect to the information, products, services, or related graphics contained in this book for any purpose. Any use of this information is at your own risk. The author has made every effort to ensure the accuracy of the information within this book was correct at time of publication. The publisher and author do not assume and hereby disclaims any liability to any party for any loss, damage, or disruption caused by errors or omissions, whether such errors or omissions result from accident, negligence, or any other cause.

All rights reserved. No part of this publication may be reproduced, distributed, or transmitted in any form or by any means, including photocopying, recording, or other electronic or mechanical methods, without the prior written permission of the publisher, except in the case of brief quotations embodied in critical reviews and certain other noncommercial uses permitted by copyright law. For permission requests, write to the publisher, addressed "Attention: Permissions Coordinator," at the address below.

Design Community College Inc.
PO Box 1153
Topanga CA 90290 USA
info@dcc-edu.org
Designed and illustrated by Robert Curedale
Cover color graphic and artwork designed by Robert Curedale
ISBN-10: 1-940805-50-3
ISBN-13: 978-1-940805-50-4

AFFINITY DIAGRAMS
STEP-BY-STEP GUIDE
2ND EDITION

ROBERT CUREDALE

PUBLISHED BY DESIGN COMMUNITY COLLEGE INC.
LOS ANGELES https://dcc-edu.org

CONTENTS

INTRODUCTION

01 APPLYING MAPPING METHODS IN YOUR ORGANIZATION 08
1. Moderating groups
2. Roles
3. Assistant moderator
4. Moderator
5. Group behavior
6. Constructive group behaviors
7. Destructive group behaviors
8. Intervention
9. Time management
10. Keep the interview on track
11. What methods did you use to research your customers?
12. Which internal departments were represented in your mapping team?
13. Use the interview guide
14. Do not rush the discussion
15. Moderator skills
16. Building rapport
17. Listening to discussion participants
18. Teams
19. Diversity
20. Who sponsored your most recent mapping project?
21. Empowerment
22. Facilitation
23. Which research method was most effective for journey mapping?
24. Collective intelligence
25. Which software tools have you used to create journey maps?
26. Cross pollination
27. Cross-disciplinary collaboration
28. Everyone contributes
29. What methods did you use to research your customers?

02 DESIGN PROCESS OVERVIEW 34
1. The design phases
2. Process map
3. The double diamond process model

03 DISCOVERY 43
1. The discovery process
2. Bias
3. Research plan
4. Question matrix
5. Activity map
6. Anthropump
7. Behavioral map
8. Benchmarking

9. Benefits map
10. Boundary shifting
11. Camera journal
12. Open card sort
13. Closed card sort
14. Benchmarking matrix
15. For product design
16. Day in the life
17. Dot voting
18. Emotion cards
19. Five whys
20. Fly-on-the-wall
21. Focus groups
22. Ideation decision matrix
23. Consensus matrix
24. Interviews
25. Planning interviews
26. Challenges
27. Planning
28. Conducting the interview
29. Interview guide
30. Problem definition
31. Problem interview script
32. Welcome
33. Background information
34. Tell a story
35. Problem ranking
36. Customer's world view
37. Wrap-up
38. Document results
39. Interview guide
40. Interview consent form
41. Interviewing methods

- Contextual inquiry
- Group interview
- Guided storytelling
- Man in the street
- Naturalistic group
- One-on-one interview
- Structured interview
- Photo elicitation
- Unstructured interview
- Telephone interview

42. Mixed method research
43. Observation
- Covert observation
- Direct observation
- Indirect observation
- Non-participant
- Participant observation
- Overt observation
- Structured observation

44. User stories
45. What-how-why method
46. WWWWWH

04 AFFINITY DIAGRAMS   104

05 GLOSSARY   118

06 INDEX   136

07 COURSES & OTHER TITLES   146

1. Other DCC titles
2. About the Author

20TH CENTURY DESIGN | 21ST CENTURY DESIGN

INDIVIDUAL DESIGNERS

DESIGN TEAMS

PRODUCTS

SYSTEMS OF PRODUCTS, SERVICES AND EXPERIENCES

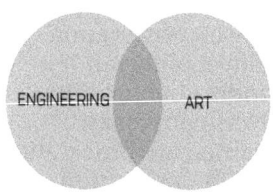

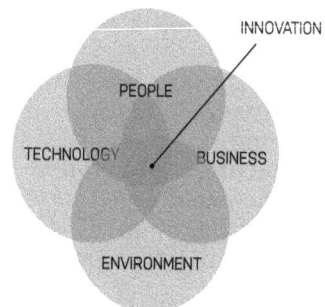

DESIGN INSPIRATION FROM IMAGES OF THE WORK OF 20 FAMOUS DESIGNERS IN EACH DESIGN DISCIPLINE

DESIGN INSPIRATION FROM RESEARCH AND THE UNMET NEEDS OF-END USERS

3D DESIGN SKILLS
SKETCHING
MODELMAKING
CAD

4D DESIGN SKILLS
IDENTIFYING UNMET NEEDS
EXPERIENCE MAPS
SERVICE BLUEPRINTS
INTERVIEWING
SCENARIOS
CO-DESIGN
VALUE NETWORKS

INTRODUCTION

The problems that designers are addressing are becoming more complex. Designers and managers are processing more information to reach better decisions. Affinity diagrams are one of the best tools to go from data chaos and being overwhelmed with too much information to identifying the best solution to a problem. Affinity diagrams help prioritize actions and improve group decision-making . Whether you're brainstorming ideas, or dealing with lots of information from a variety of sources, you can struggle to make sense out of the information. A brainstorming session or a series of customer interviews may generate hundreds of ideas or pieces of data. They can help you process large bodies of information, facts, ethnographic research, ideas from brainstorms, user opinions, user needs, and insights. An affinity diagram is one of the most efficient ways of deciding what is most important so that a favored design solution can then be prototyped and tested. Affinity diagrams, sometimes called the KJ method, are one of the most useful tools for organizing information or ideas into groups so that effective and efficient decisions can be made. The word "affinity" refers to the natural connections among ideas. The method was first developed by Kawakita Jiro a brilliant Japanese anthropologist in the 1950s and 1960s. It may be the single most significant advance in design practice made in design over the last half century. Without affinity diagrams it would be difficult to work in any environment where designers need to make sense of complex data. The Japanese Union of Scientists and Engineers consider affinity diagrams one of the "seven key management tools" used in Total Quality Control in Japan. From the chaos of the randomly generated ideas emerge insights into the connections and significance of ideas. The affinity process is one of the best ways of making sense of ideas generated during a brainstorming session. This tool can be used in any phase of the design process. Two common uses are problem and solution identification. It is also often used in contextual inquiry to process research data and insights from field interviews. It can be used for synthesizing survey responses or other research data. Affinity diagrams encourage full team participation in the development of more people-centered solutions. They can be used in any situation where the solution is not initially apparent or where you want to reach a consensus and have a lot of variables to consider. Here is a step-by-step guide to using affinity diagrams. I hope that you will find it useful. You can find many more guides and online courses related to emerging design and innovation on my web site www.dcc-edu.org.

APPLYING AFFINITY DIAGRAMS IN YOUR ORGANIZATION

APPLYING EMPATHY MAPPING IN YOUR ORGANIZATION

Here is some advice to help you introduce design thinking into your organization.

FIRST LEARN ABOUT DESIGN THINKING
Arrange for several leaders in your organization representing the main cross-functional departments to do a substantial course in design thinking together.

GIVE EVERYONE A VOICE
Invite everyone to a series of meetings to discuss the introduction of design thinking in your organization.

LEAVE YOUR OFFICE AND EXPERIENCE YOUR CUSTOMER'S WORLD
Listen to your customers to understand what their problems are. Don't solve the wrong problem because you are remote from your customers.

COLLABORATE
Define the goals together as a team with everyone's input.

WHEN YOU HAVE A PRELIMINARY DESIGN GET FEEDBACK FROM CUSTOMERS
Share the designs as widely as possible with internal and external stakeholders and invite their feedback.

LEARN BY FAILING AND TRYING AGAIN
It is important to understand that if you are trying new things not every design idea will be successful. Use the methods in this book to minimize the cost of inevitable failures during prototyping and experimentation.

INVITE ALL DEPARTMENTS AND EXTERNAL STAKEHOLDERS TO YOUR WORKSHOPS
You should have one team composed of stakeholders with different perspectives.

CHOOSE THE TEAM MEMBERS IN YOUR GROUPS CAREFULLY
Four to eight people is an optimum groups size. If you have a larger group break it into smaller groups. Consider diversity and personalities when forming groups. Don't put several people with strong personalities into the same group. Create space for discussion where people feel safe.

START WITH A MANAGEABLE DESIGN PROBLEM
Run several small-scale design thinking exercises before taking on a larger project.

> *Because we invested in building innovation skills into our employee base, we are not only a design-thinking company, we're a design-driven company. Meaning, we're going from creating a culture of design thinking to building a practice of design doing, where we relentlessly focus on nailing the end-to-end customer experience. This means that before anything gets built, the whole team engineers, designers, marketers, product managers are interfacing with the customers to ensure they understand the problem well, and together, they design the best solution."*
>
> Suzanne Pellican,
> Vice President Of Experience Design at Intuit

EMPATHY IS NOT THE SAME AS HUMAN FACTORS
Design thinking tools consider not just usability issues but also people's emotions, attitudes, and values.

THINK HOLISTICALLY
Analytical thinkers can sometimes focus on the small details rather than the bigger issues. The process of design thinking will allow you to consider both. Think about design problems systematically, products, services, and experiences. How are these things connected?

LOOK FOR UNMET NEEDS
Consider and involve the customer at every stage.

BUILD UP YOUR SOLUTIONS
Prototype early and learn and build up the solution by asking questions.

CONSIDER THE CUSTOMER JOURNEY NOT JUST THE DESTINATION
The customer journey consists of a series of micro-experiences. Design thinking tools allow you to consider and optimize each of these moments to build a better overall experience.

BUILD A WAR ROOM
Place all your research and all your ideas on a wall where everyone in tour team can see it and think about and discuss what may be relevant and connected. Keep one space dedicated to your project for the entire project. Pick a large space with natural light.

GIVE PEOPLE DEFINED TIMES FOR EACH ACTIVITY
Don't give them too much time. 30-minutes to generate ideas, 15 minutes for discussion, 20-minutes to make a fast prototype. Keep the activities focused and moving. Have clear goals with each team activity.

MODERATING GROUPS

If you have the resources have two people moderate. The moderator can facilitate the group discussion while the assistant moderator takes notes and looks after the video camera. Moderating a team activity successfully is a skill which is partly a talent and partly developed through experience.

ROLES

1. **Facilitator.** The person who moderates the group.
2. **Recorder.** The person who captures the discussion
3. **Data Analyst.** The person who analyses the notes or recordings of the group discussion
4. **Report Writer.** The person who writes executive summary of the discussions.
5. **Scheduler.** The person who schedules the meetings.
6. **Manager of Logistics.** The person who manages the room and other logistics.

ASSISTANT MODERATOR

1. Manages the equipment and refreshments
2. Arranges the room
3. Manages video camera and other recording equipment
4. Welcome participants as they arrive
5. Has good listening skills
6. Has good observation skills
7. Has good writing skills
8. Acts as an observer, not as a participant
9. Can remain impartial
10. Take notes throughout the discussion
11. Notes should include observation of non-verbal behavior
12. Notes should include themes, follow-up questions, body language, confusion, nonverbal communication, facial expressions, gestures, signs of agreement, disagreement, frustration, and participant concerns, head nods, physical excitement, eye contact between participants, or other clues that would indicate level of support, or interest.
13. Notes follow-up questions that could be asked
14. The assistant moderator does not get involved in the group discussion.
15. Assistant should be a "fly on the wall" and only observe the discussion.
16. Should not influence the discussion by their presence.
17. Provides participant seating arrangement
18. Operate recording equipment
19. Do not participate in the discussion
20. Ask questions when invited
21. Give an oral summary
22. Debrief with moderator
23. Give feedback on analysis and reports
24. Can Handle logistics & refreshments
25. Collects signed informed

consent (if required)
26. Takes careful notes
27. Does not participate in discussion
28. Can recap major themes at end of discussion (used before wrap-up question)
29. Monitors recording equipment
30. Liaison between moderator and observers/clients
31. Debriefs with moderator after session
32. Assist with analysis and reports
33. Not required, but can be useful in some situations
34. Balance out strengths/weaknesses in moderator
35. Use to match moderator (without being obvious)
36. Switch leading discussion (good for long or intense discussions)
37. Support leader by keeping on track, recapping major themes, etc.

MODERATOR

Select the moderator carefully.
1. Someone who is culturally like the people participating.
2. Manages the process of the discussion rather than the content.
3. The moderator should have empathy with the group but also have authority.
4. Does not need to be an expert on the discussion topic but needs to show skill in managing discussion.
5. Should not share views,
6. Probes the discussion points to reveal the underlying reasons.
7. Should 'Warm up' the group to help participants feel at ease,
8. Should develop rapport with the participants.
9. Needs to stay focused.
10. Should ensure that all participants are involved in the discussion.
11. Spends the minimum time necessary speaking.
12. Should not show bias.
13. Directs the discussion in real time
14. Follows the question guide.
15. Have an assistant to take notes and manage equipment and time.
16. The moderator should have good listening skills.
17. Use an experienced moderator.
18. A person able to create and manage a friendly and participatory environment.
19. Use pauses and probes
20. Probes:
    - "Can you explain further?"
    - "Could you give an example?"
21. Manage participants
    - Verbal and nonverbal communication
    - Short responses
    - Experts
    - Dominant talkers
    - Shy participants
    - Ramblers
22. The moderator should remain neutral and not show extremes of emotion such as surprise or anger during the conversation.

23. The moderator should be diplomatic.
24. The moderator prevents some participants from dominating the conversation.
25. Can clearly summarize and articulate the views expressed.
26. Do not let the discussion stray into areas that are emotionally charged.

GROUP BEHAVIOR

CONSTRUCTIVE GROUP BEHAVIORS
1. Collaboration. The members of the group are interested and listen to the views of other participants.
2. Clarifies points. Asks questions in order to understand ambiguous ideas.
3. Inspires the group with relevant examples.
4. Harmony. Works to build group cohesion
5. Takes risks. Sticks their neck out to achieve the goals.
6. Reviews the process so they properly understand the goals, agenda, schedule and other points.

DESTRUCTIVE GROUP BEHAVIORS
1. Dominates the conversation with one opinion.
2. Wants to move on before the discussion is complete.
3. Does not participate in the discussion.
4. Discounts or ridicules other opinions.
5. Loses focus on the topic or goals.
6. Blocks unfamiliar ideas.
7. Self-Appointed Experts. Thank them for their knowledge and redirect question to the rest of the group
8. If one participant tries to dominate the session, the moderator should invite each person to speak in turn.
9. Shy Participants. Respect someone's right to be quiet, but do give them a chance to share their ideas
10. Ramblers. Intervene, politely summarize and refocus. Use nonverbal cues; redirect.
11. Side Talking/Side Conversation. Remind the group or individuals about the ground rules

INTERVENTION
A good moderator will intervene in the discussion when necessary Establish the ground rules in the introduction. This gives common expectations so that the team members can help manage people who exhibit destructive behavior. Listen to each person's ideas. Ask questions to clarify points or reveal bias.

1. Break a large group into smaller groups of 4 people.
2. Remind the group of the task.
3. Take a break and speak to a disruptive participant about the goals.
4. Break the problem into

smaller parts.
5. Define a way to make decisions.
6. List the areas of agreement.

TIME MANAGEMENT
It is important that time is planned and managed well so that all the topics can be covered.

KEEP THE INTERVIEW ON TRACK
One of the important skills for a moderator is to steer the conversation back to the topic if it strays and to move on from question to question.

USE THE INTERVIEW GUIDE
Write in prompts to remind you to check the time at several points during the discussion.

DO NOT RUSH THE DISCUSSION
Interrupt as little as possible and not rush them.
1. Have good listening skills
2. Have good observation skills
3. Have good speaking skills
4. Can foster open and honest dialogue among diverse groups and individuals
5. Can remain impartial (i.e., do not give her/his opinions about topics, because
6. This can influence what people say)
7. Can encourage participation when someone is reluctant to speak up
8. Can manage participants who dominate the conversation
9. Are sensitive to gender and cultural issues
10. Are sensitive to differences in power among and within groups.

MODERATOR SKILLS
BUILDING RAPPORT
1. Building rapport is important.
2. Show the participants that you are a person who is prepared and willing to listen to them with interest.
3. Let the participants know that you are there to learn from them.
4. It is important to present yourself as someone facilitating rather than as a friend.
5. Balance rapport and professionalism.

LISTENING TO INTERVIEW AND DISCUSSION PARTICIPANTS
The guidelines for conducting interviews and discussions are closely connected to building rapport. These guidelines include communicating to the participants that you are listening to them as well as these strategies: neutrality, silence, and guidance.
6. Show participants that you are listening.
7. Stay neutral.
8. You want to gather information that is as honest as possible.
9. Silence is acceptable. Asking clarifying questions. Guidance includes giving
10. Monitor time carefully.

TEAMS

History demonstrates that great projects and products are often the result of great teams.

Start with a clear goal and a serious deadline.
A hot group is infused with purpose and personality.
If you distrust the power of teamwork, consider this fact. Even the most legendary individual inventor is often a team in disguise. In six scant years, for example, Thomas Edison generated an astounding four hundred patents. producing: innovations in the telegraph. telephone phonograph, and lightbulb- with the help of a fourteen-man team. As Francis Jehl, Edison's longtime assistant, explained, "Edison is in reality a collective noun and means the work of many men." The same is often true of the lone genius within a company. We've found that loners are so caught up in their idea that they are reluctant to let it go, much less allow it to be experimented with and improved upon.

The right kinds of specializations are important, but specialization is not the only quality required. To make a Design Thinking project successful, we need T-shaped people. T-shaped people have a depth of knowledge and experience in their own fields but they can also reach out and connect with others horizontally and create meaningful collaborations.

WORKING WITH TEAMS

1. The team should have a common vision. Write that vision and display it prominently in the workspace. Refer back to the vision statement when decisions are being made to ensure that they are consistent with the vision.
2. Adopt and work with common values and rules such as the brainstorming rules.
3. Share common precesses.
4. Work together in one space.
5. Promote an atmosphere of trust and acceptance where people feel safe to put forward their ideas.
6. Encourage two way communication with feedback.

DIVERSITY

Each team member brings their unique perspective and expertise to the team, widening the range of possible outcomes. If you want a breakthrough idea, you're more likely to get it with a diverse team. Diverse teams see the same problem from many angles. They have a better understanding of any given situation and generate more ideas, making them more effective problem solvers. While it takes effort to harness and align such different perspectives, it's at the intersection of our differences that our most meaningful breakthroughs emerge.

Cross-disciplinary teams will provide you with the best results. Teams may consist of people unfamiliar with each other, with external members brought on board either as specialists or facilitators depending on the availability of skills.

IDENTITY
1. Age and ability
2. Gender identity
3. Race and ethnicity

EXPERIENCE
1. Cultural upbringing
2. Geography
3. Language

EXPERTISE
1. Education
2. Organization
3. Discipline

Source:IBM

The right kinds of specializations are important, but specialization is not the only quality required. To make a Design Thinking project successful, we need T-shaped people. T-shaped people have a depth of knowledge and experience in their own fields but they can also reach out and connect with others horizontally and create meaningful collaborations.

A Design Thinking team should ideally be a cross/multi-disciplinary team consisting of a mix of specializations, including specialists associated with problem areas contributing but not dominating the journey. While specialists may have vast knowledge on a technical level, they are working towards solutions targeted towards non-specialists in many cases and require outside perspectives in addition to what they already know.

EMPOWERMENT
Teams should be equipped with the expertise and independence to deliver outcomes without relying on others for decisions or technical support.

Grant them the authority to handle day-to-day activities on the team and hold them accountable for achieving their assigned outcome.

FACILITATION
1. Start with a clear goal and a serious deadline
2. Explain the five stages of the Design Thinking Process.
3. Provide your team members with printed out models of the Design Thinking process and modes to help them understand and recognize the benefits of the Design Thinking work process.
4. Explain how Design Thinking builds a third way – combining the analytical and information-driven approach of science with the holistic, empathic and creative ways of thinking in ethnography and design.
5. Explain that there are lots of proven methods
6. Knowing the background and underlying structure will help your team members to

feel safer as they know that there's a solid background
7. Bring together a diverse team with different thinking styles and specializations.
8. Develop an innovative team culture, which embraces inclusiveness, collaboration, and co-creation.
9. Level the playing field to allow for a diverse set of perspectives to influence the process.
10. Ensure the right person is in charge.
11. Break the ice with some creative exercises to loosen things up.

> *One must still have chaos in oneself to be able to give birth to a dancing star."*
> Friedrich Nietzsche

CONFLICT

Diversity invites conflict— and conflict is a wellspring of creativity. Harnessing this creativity requires us to listen to understand, not just argue, with those who may disagree. When you listening to understand, you uncover brand new ideas together and contribute to a more open and collaborative culture."

"Empathy: first with each other. Then with our users."

IBM

1. Instinct often leads us to avoid conflict and seek out those who think alike.
2. At minimum, critical team conversations should include representatives from every discipline affected. It would be unwise for engineering to make timeline decision without engaging offering management in a conversation, or for product designers to make brand decisions without consulting the marketing team.
3. This kind of radical collaboration requires a foundation of trust, respect, and shared ownership across the team.

Edison is, in reality, a collective noun and means the work of many men."

Francis Jehl
Edison's assistant

Which skills and mindsets do team players need for a design project?

1. Openness: smell, touch, taste, observe, listen, ask, hear, feel...
2. Able to find the right questions.

APPLYING AFFINITY DIAGRAMS IN YOUR ORGANIZATION

3. Able to suspend your judgment and look beyond the obvious.
4. Able to understand different points of view,
5. See the big picture and create common grounds.
6. Able to imagine and build solutions haven't seen before.
7. Able to create cheap experiments in order to learn faster."

D Osterwalder,
Anna Ploskonos

COLLECTIVE INTELLIGENCE

Collective intelligence is a type of shared intelligence that emerges from the collaboration of many people and is expressed in consensus decision-making.

Collective intelligence requires four conditions to exist.
1. Openness Sharing ideas, experiences and perspectives
2. Peering people are free to share and build on each other's ideas freely.
3. Sharing knowledge, experiences ideas.
4. Acting globally

CROSS POLLINATION

Use cross-disciplinary teams. Share ideas and observations with people outside your organization. Travel can help your design team get exposed to new ways of looking at a problem. Read outside your field. Talk to people in different industries.

CROSS-DISCIPLINARY COLLABORATION

Depending on the design challenge, design teams can engage anthropologists, engineers, educators, doctors, lawyers, scientists, etc. in the innovative problem-solving process. Everyone can contribute. The Design Thinking process involves many stakeholders in working together. The designer is a member of the orchestra. The customer is involved throughout the design process and works with the design team to communicate their needs and desires and to help generate design solutions that are relevant to them.

The process is one of co-creation and the designer is a listener and a facilitator. Everyone adds value to the design. Design thinking is not just for professional designers. Everyone can contribute. Many schools are now teaching Design Thinking to children as an approach that can be applied to life.

STYLES OF FEEDBACK

TRADITIONAL ENVIRONMENT	DESIGN THINKING APPROACH
Criticism finds fault	Critique uncovers opportunity
Criticism is personal	Critique is objective
Criticism is vague	Critique is concrete
Criticism tears down	Critique builds up
Criticism is ego-centric	Critique is altruistic
Criticism is adversarial	Critique is cooperative
Criticism belittles the designer	Critique improves the design

Source *Writing Alone, Writing Together; A Guide for Writers and Writing Groups* by Judy Reeves

BREAKING DOWN SILOS
Many organizations struggle to break down the barriers that prevent them from innovating. One of those barriers is the silo mentality where departments do not share information or effectively collaborate. Culture, language, and time zone differences compound the effects of organizational silos. Activities are uncoordinated and duplicative.

In organizations with silos teams work against each other. Breaking down silos starts the people you are hiring. Overcoming organizational silos requires supportive departmental structures, processes, reward mechanisms, reporting structures, furniture selection and office layouts. Siloed teams struggle to solve problems.

In siloed organizations employees follow vertical career paths, staying within one functional group or department.

CREATE ONE ORGANIZATIONAL VISION.
Align leaders to ensure that the leadership team agrees to a common unified vision for the organization. A unified leadership team will build trust in one vision.

WORK TOWARDS ACHIEVING A COMMON GOAL.
First identify existing multiple tactical goals and objectives. Build one unified vision and ensure that all employees are aware of this objective and understand how they can make an impact individually.

CREATE CROSS-FUNCTIONAL TEAMS.
Create clear roles and responsibilities.

INCENTIVIZE.
To motivate team members use common interests, individual investment in growth, shared voice, and positive words of encouragement. Create joint incentives. Request joint deliverables and metrics. Ensure that reviews and bonuses tie everyone to one strategic vision.

JOINT GOVERNANCE FORUM
Create a body with representatives from every department to meet together regularly to debate challenges, issues, and trade-offs, to support your common vision.

METRICS
Managers should establish a time frame to complete the common goal, benchmarks for success and delegate specific tasks and objectives to members of the team.

CO-LOCATE
Global teams have limited time together and complex communication issues. Co-locate teams where possible.
Since the need for Keep teams in the same physical location and have multidisciplinary teams rather than having all the engineers in one room and all the marketing people in another room or building.

CO-LEADERS
Appoint two leaders for "two in a box" style leadership. This will build improved accountability and collaboration.

Design thinking is, then, always linked to an improved future. Unlike critical thinking, which is a process of analysis and is associated with the 'breaking down' of ideas, design thinking is a creative process based around the 'building up' of ideas. There are no judgments in design thinking. This eliminates the fear of failure and encourages maximum input and participation. Wild ideas are welcome, since these often lead to the most creative solutions. Everyone is a designer, and design thinking is a way to apply design methodologies to any of life's situations.

Herbert Simon

INNOVATION DIAGNOSTIC

WHAT

An innovation diagnostic is an evaluation of an organization's innovation capabilities. It reviews practices by stakeholders which may help or hinder innovation. An innovation diagnostic is the first step in preparing and implementing a strategy to create an organizational culture that supports innovation. Before you start to research your audience. Do a diagnostic of your organization to find out how you can remove obstacles to innovation. Do an exercise to help get your team up to speed working.

WHY

1. It helps organizations develop sustainable competitive advantage
2. Helps identify innovation opportunities
3. Helps develop innovation strategy.
4. Evaluate structural weaknesses in an organization that may be limiting that organization's ability to innovate.

HOW

An innovation diagnostic reviews organizational and stakeholder practices using both qualitative and quantitative methods including

1. The design and development process
2. Strategic practices and planning
3. The ability of an organization to monitor and respond to relevant trends.
4. Technologies
5. Organizational flexibility
6. Ability to innovate repeatedly and consistently

SELF-QUESTIONNAIRE

Answer these questions and score yourself to understand to what degree your organization OR your client's organization supports innovation.

DOES MANAGEMENT COMMUNICATE THE NEED FOR INNOVATION?

1. There is no innovation in our organization
2. Innovation is not a high priority
3. Our managers sometimes talk about innovation
4. Our managers discuss innovation but not why it is needed
5. Managers regularly state the compelling need for

innovation

WHAT IS YOUR ORGANIZATIONAL STRATEGY?
1. We make low-cost goods or services
2. Efficient operations
3. We are a customer focused organization
4. Fast Follower
5. Market leaders

IS THE BUSINESS THAT YOU ARE IN UNDERSTOOD BY EMPLOYEES?
1. We are not sure
2. We may get different answers from different managers
3. The definition changes in
4. We have some clarity
5. We are very clear about what business we are in

IS YOUR ORGANIZATION INNOVATIVE?
1. No
2. Probably not
3. We would like to be
4. There is some innovation
5. We are clearly an innovative organization

HOW DOES YOUR COMPANY INNOVATE?
1. We react to market forces without innovation
2. There is little innovation
3. We do some incremental innovation
4. We do mainly incremental innovation but would like to do some breakthrough innovation
5. We manage a portfolio of incremental and more substantial innovation and manage risks

DOES YOUR MANAGEMENT SUPPORT INNOVATION?
1. No
2. No resources are allocated to innovation
3. Some resources are allocated
4. We have some resources and some involvement from managers in innovation
5. We have clearly defined resources allocated and senior management is actively involved in planning and managing innovation

DO YOU HAVE CROSS-DISCIPLINARY DESIGN TEAMS?
1. Never
2. Rarely
3. Sometimes
4. Usually
5. Always

DO YOU USE OUTSIDE EXPERTS TO ASSIST IN YOUR INNOVATION PROCESS?
1. Never
2. Rarely
3. Sometimes
4. Usually
5. Always

HOW OFTEN DOES YOUR ORGANIZATION ENGAGE CUSTOMERS TO IDENTIFY THEIR UNMET NEEDS?
1. Never
2. Rarely

3. Sometimes
4. Usually
5. Always

HOW WOULD YOU DEFINE THE RISK TOLERANCE AT YOUR COMPANY?

1. We don't take any risks
2. We rarely take risks
3. Sometimes we take substantial risks
4. We manage our risk portfolio actively and take big risks when appropriate.

HOW ARE NEW IDEAS RECEIVED IN YOUR ORGANIZATION?

1. We fire people with new ideas
2. We rarely adopt new ideas
3. We sometimes adopt new ideas but they are mostly not considered
4. We regularly consider new ideas
5. We actively generate and adopt new ideas

Add up the numbers of each answer that you selected and calculate a total for all the questions.

> **Everything is now subject to innovation, not just physical objects, but also political systems, economic policy, ways in which medical research is conducted, and even complete "user experiences."**
>
> Laura Weiss,
> IDEO

HOW WELL DID YOU SCORE?

SCORE 0 TO 15

Small changes, low investment, low risk and low return. Changing the color of a product. Every company is capable of gaining this score.

SCORE 15 TO 25

You are integrating new features into existing products and services to build differentiated versions of the same new product to sell to various demographic groups. These new features require what can be considered a medium level of investment and risk. Advancement of existing products, medium investment, and risk, medium payoff.

SCORE 25 TO 35

INNOVATIVE ORGANIZATION

The second level is the beginning of large financial and product risk, but it is also where the rewards are potentially larger. This level also requires that the business devote resources to monitoring progress and actively assessing risk throughout the development process. Evolutionary products, large investment, medium risk, some payoff.

SCORE 35 TO 45

HIGHLY INNOVATIVE ORGANIZATION

Your company has the innovation skills to change people's lives. Companies in this category have the highest level of risks you are creating products or services that are new and original. Revolutionary products and services, large investment, big risks high payoff

CHAPTER SUMMARY

INTRODUCING AFFINITY DIAGRAMS AT YOUR ORGANIZATION
1. First learn about design thinking
2. Give everyone a voice
3. Leave your office and immerse yourself in your customer's world.
4. Collaborate.
5. When you have a preliminary design get feedback from customers.
6. Do not punish failure.
7. Invite all departments and external stakeholders to your workshops.
8. Choose the team members in your groups carefully.
9. Start with a manageable design problem.
10. Empathy is not the same as human factors.
11. Think holistically.
12. Look for unmet needs.
13. Build up your solutions.
14. Consider the customer journey not just the destination.
15. Build a war room.
16. Give people defined times for each activity.

MODERATING ROLES
1. Facilitator. The person who moderates the group.
2. Recorder. The person who captures the discussion
3. Data Analyst – the person who analyses the notes or recordings of the group discussion
4. Report Writer. The person who writes executive summary of the discussions.
5. Scheduler. The person who schedules the meetings.
6. Manager of Logistics. The person who manages the room and other logistics.
7. Assistant moderator. The person who schedules the meetings.

REVIEW QUESTIONS
1. What should you do before you introduce design thinking to your organization?
2. How should you deal with failures on the project?
3. What should you look for from customers as part of the design thinking process?
4. What is a war room?
5. What are four roles when moderating groups?
6. What does an assistant moderator do?
7. What are four things you should consider when selecting a moderator?
8. What are four constructive group behaviors?
9. What are four destructive group behaviors?
10. How can a moderator build rapport with the group?
11. What is an innovation diagnostic?
12. When could you use an innovation diagnostic?

POOR UNDERSTANDING OF THE CUSTOMER'S PERSPECTIVE IS THE BIGGEST REASON FOR NEW PRODUCT AND SERVICE FAILURE

Source of data: Stage-gate.com

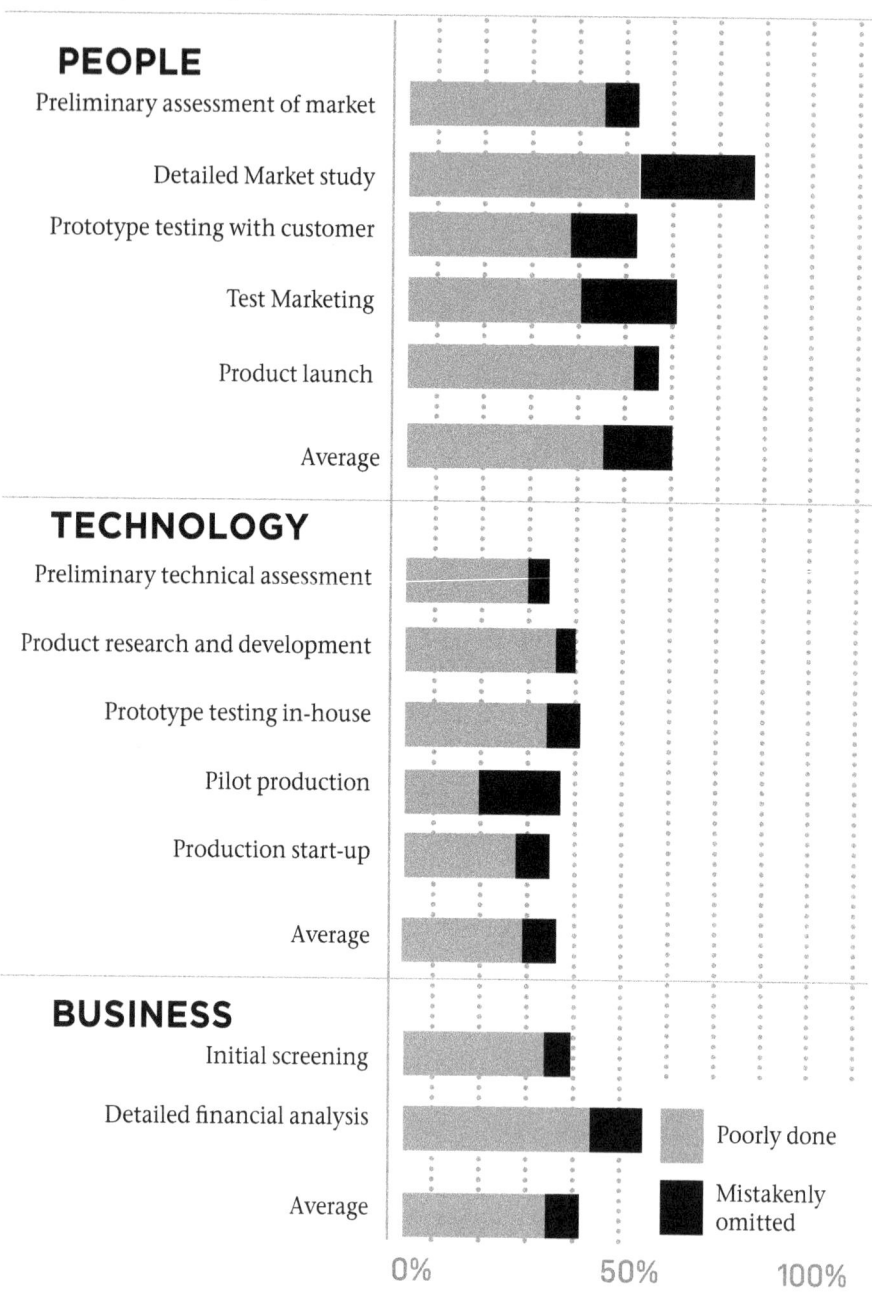

WHAT DO YOU SEE AS MOST IMPORTANT FOR SUCCESSFUL JOURNEY MAPPING?

In-house n=53 Consultants n=48

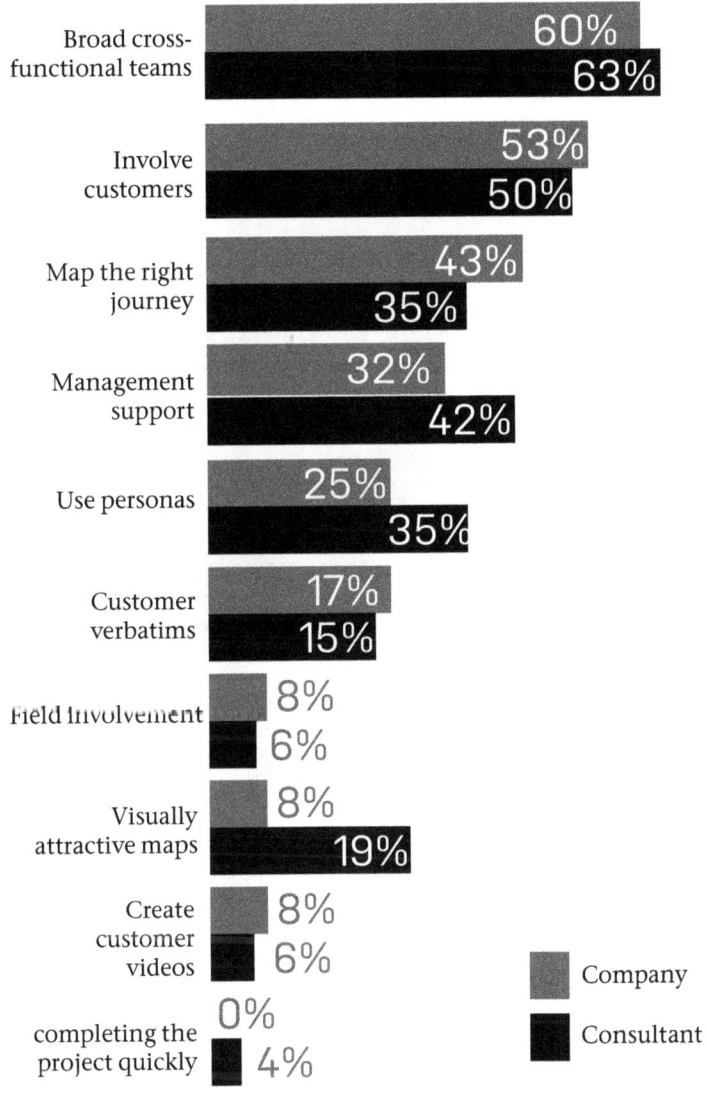

Source of data: 2016 Survey of 134 CX professionals by The Customer Experience Professionals Association and Heart of the Customer

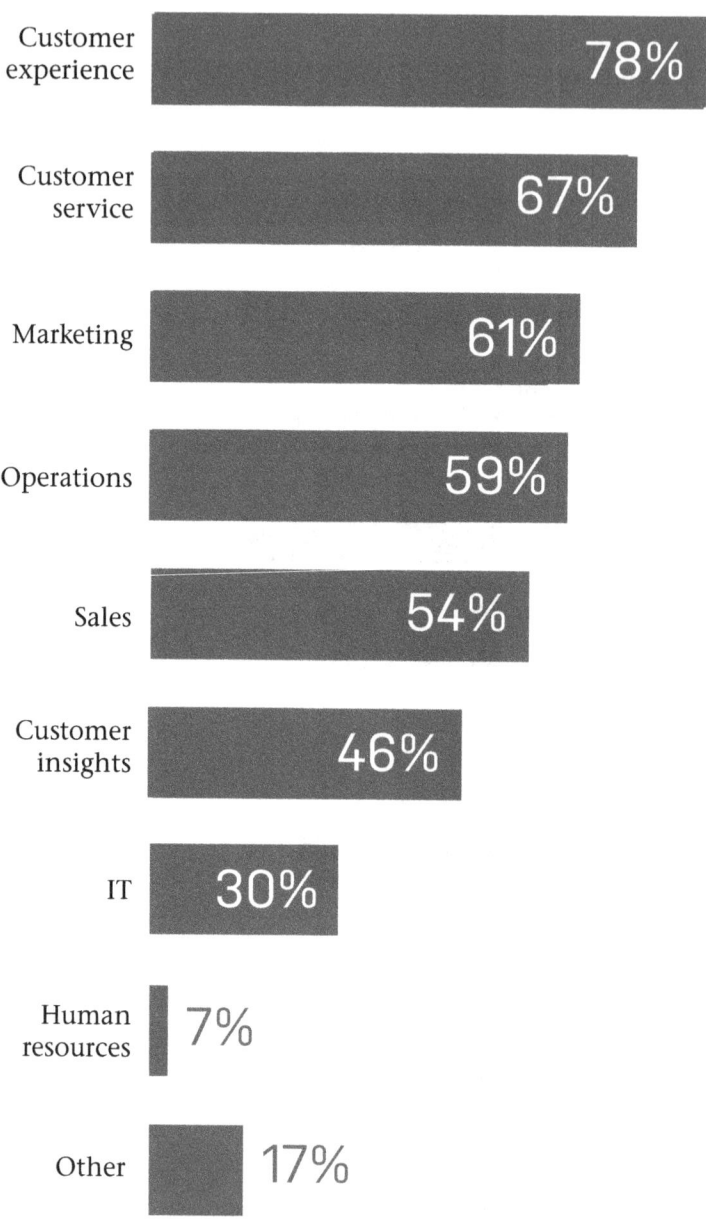

WHAT TYPE OF JOURNEY DID YOU LAST MAP?

In-house n=57

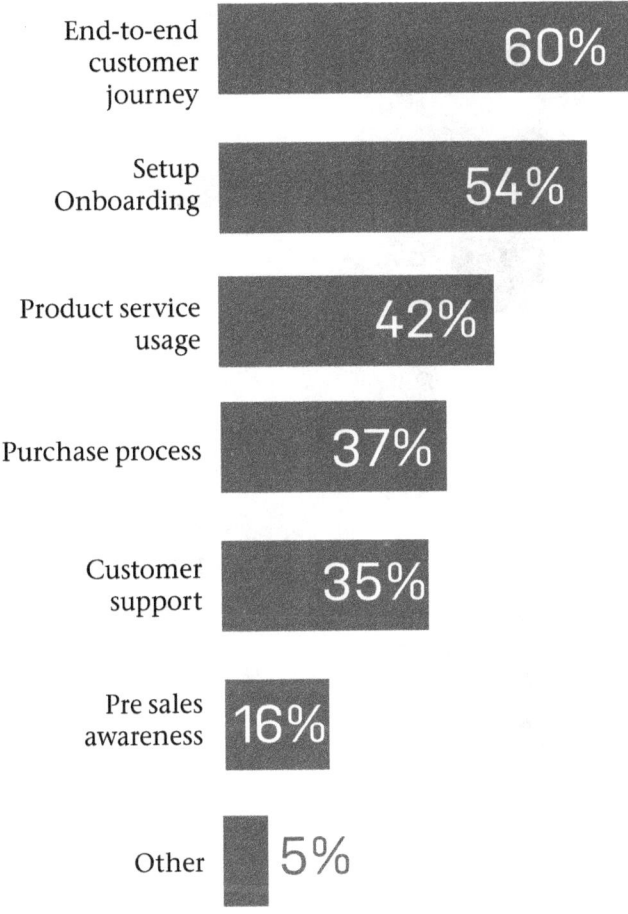

Journey type	%
End-to-end customer journey	60%
Setup Onboarding	54%
Product service usage	42%
Purchase process	37%
Customer support	35%
Pre sales awareness	16%
Other	5%

Source of data: 2016 Survey of 134 CX professionals by The Customer Experience Professionals Association and Heart of the Customer

WHO SPONSORED YOUR MOST RECENT MAPPING PROJECT?
In-house n=53

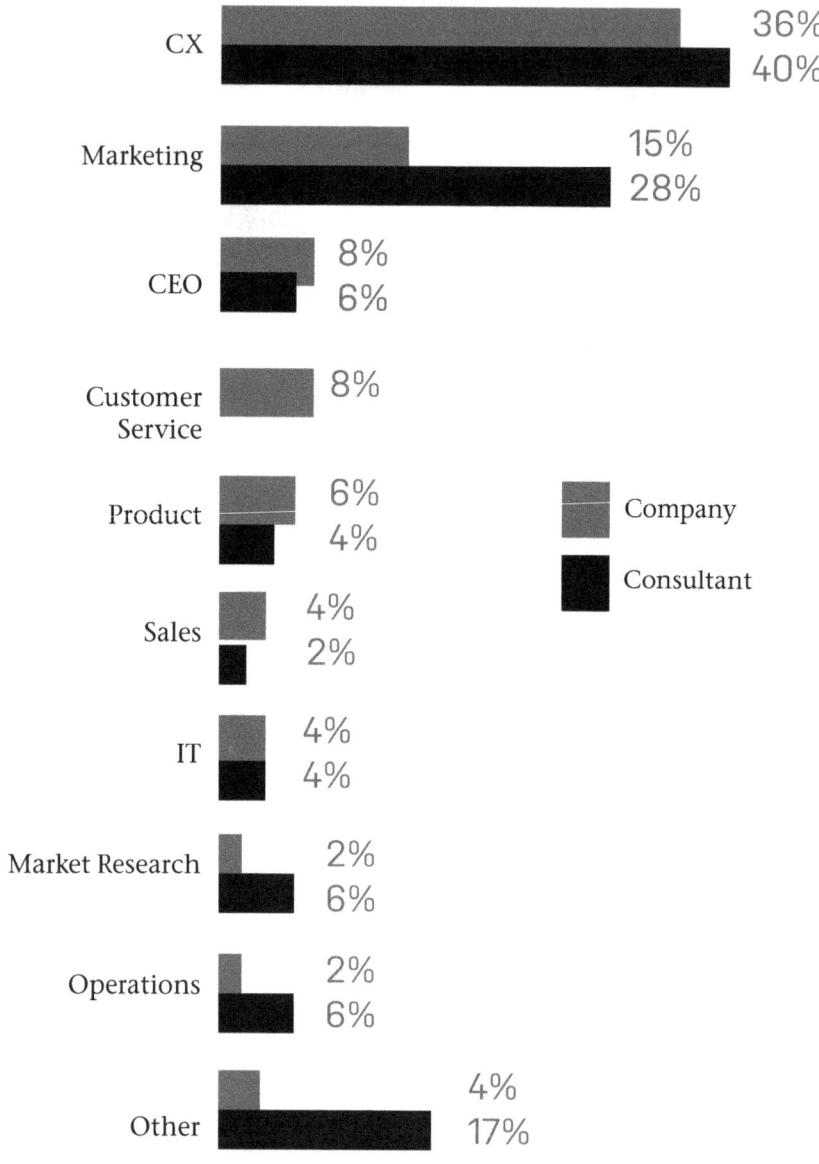

Source of data: 2016 Survey of 134 CX professionals by The Customer Experience Professionals Association and Heart of the Customer

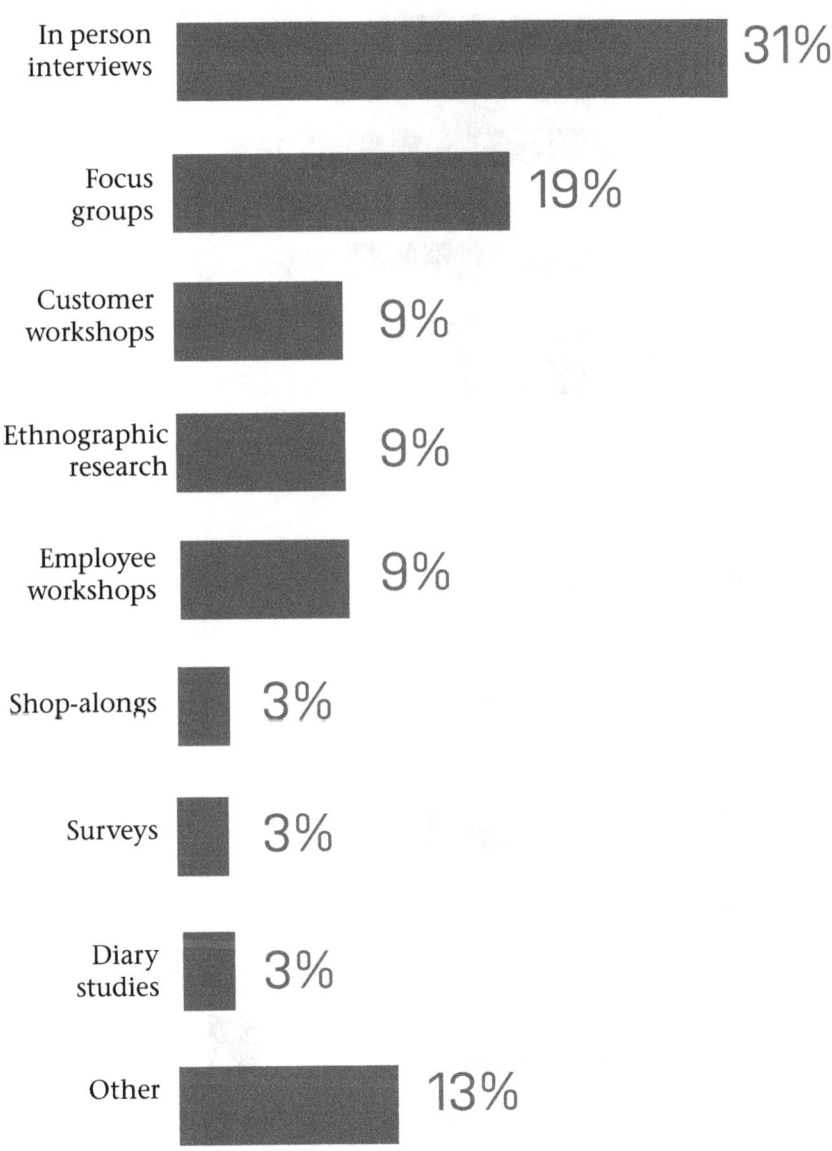

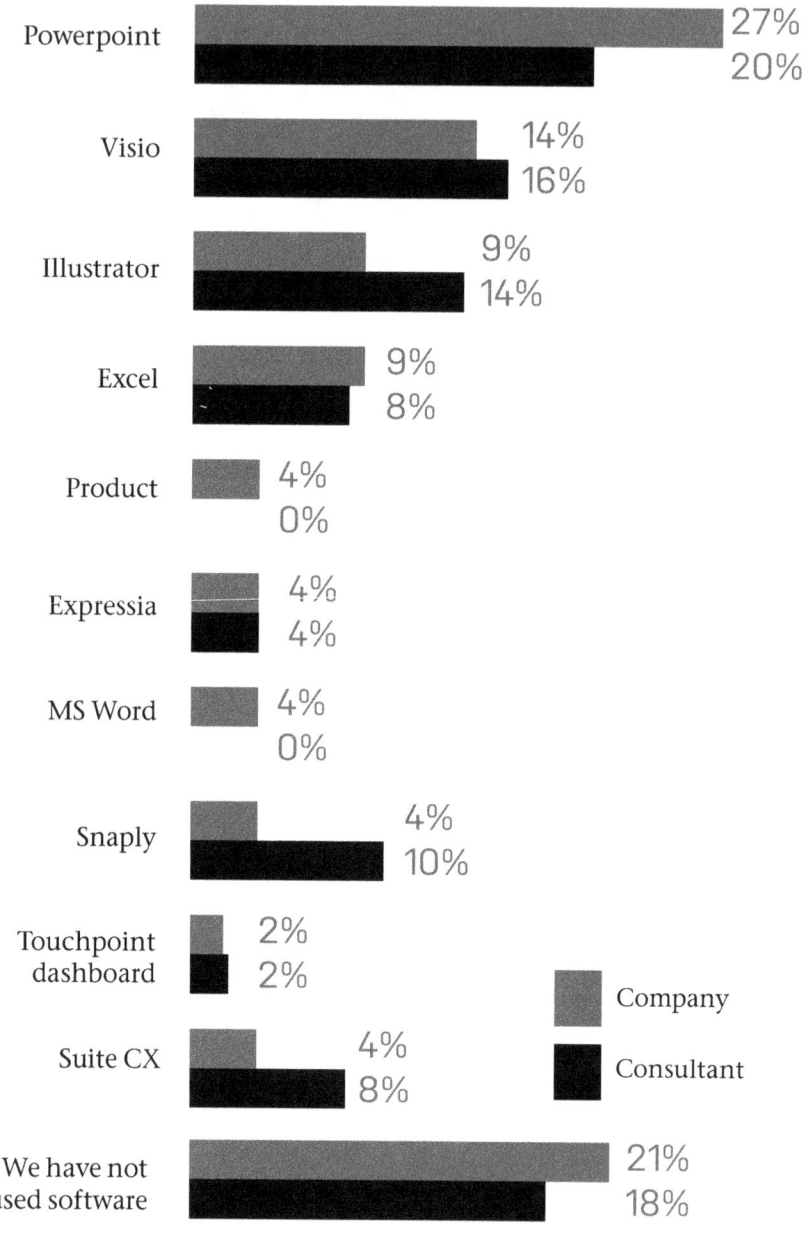

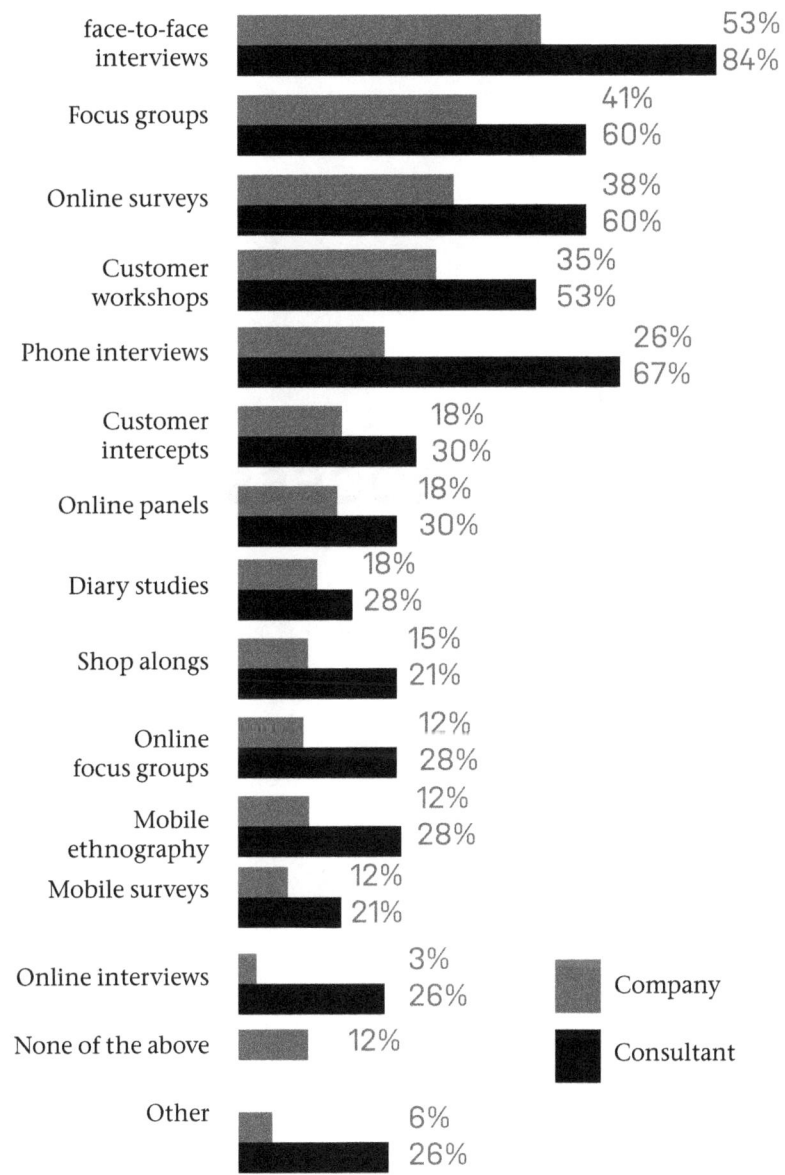

02

DESIGN PROCESS OVERVIEW

DESIGN PROCESS OVERVIEW

PLANNING
What are our goals?
1. Meet with key stakeholders to set vision and intent.
2. Assemble a diverse team
3. Explore scenarios of user experience.
4. Document stakeholders performance requirements
5. Define the group of people or user segment that you are designing for. What are their gender, age, and income range? Where do they live? What is their culture?
6. Define your scope and constraints
7. Identify a needs that you are addressing. Identify a problem that you are solving.
8. Identify opportunities.
9. Consider project risks
10. What are the main hurdles that your team will need to overcome?
11. What information do you not have that will be necessary for a successful design?
12. Create a budget and plan.
13. Create tasks and deliverables.
14. Create a schedule.

DISCOVER EMPATHIZE
What does the research tell us?
15. Identify what you know and what you need to know.
16. Document a research plan
17. Benchmark competitive products.
18. Explore the context of use
19. Understand the risks.
20. Observe and interview individuals, groups, experts.
21. Develop design strategy.
22. Undertake qualitative, quantitative, primary and secondary research.
23. Talk to vendors.

SYNTHESIZE
What have we learned?
24. Review the research.
25. Make sense out of the research.
26. Develop insights.
27. Cluster insights.
28. Create a hierarchy.

HAVE A UNIQUE POINT OF VIEW
What is the design brief?

IDEATE
How is this for as a starting point?
29. Brainstorm
30. Define the most promising ideas.
31. Refine the ideas.
32. Establish key differentiation of your ideas.

DESIGN PROCESS

| PLAN | WARM UP | DISCOVER/ RESEARCH/ EMPATHIZE | SYNTHESIS/ POINT OF VIEW |

ACTIVITIES

PLAN
Define project goals and opportunities and end users.

The goal is to understand the value of the proposed design project and some basic objectives.

WARM UP
Some fast exercises to get the team up to speed and working productively with each other.

DISCOVER
Develop a deep understanding of your customers or end users through engaging them and using ethnographic research methods. Identify stakeholder needs.

SYNTHESIS POV
Make sense from your research. What are the insights? What is connected? What are the unmet needs? What is the opportunity? Define the problem that you will solve.

METHODS

Innovation Diagnostic Smart goals Blue ocean Goal grid Reframing matrix Warming up Wwwwwh Interviews Observation Focus groups Day in the life Perceptual maps	Desert island Milestones Common Ground Hobby Barney Difficult experience Observe Compliment Free association Zombie cats	Research plan Observation Focus Groups Day in the life Diary studies Benchmarking Competitors Analysis Camera journals Empathy tools Web analytics Stakeholder interviews	Affinity diagrams 5 Whys Mind Maps Personas Perceptual Maps Empathy Maps Experience Maps Service blueprints

OUTPUT

| PROJECT PLAN | PRODUCTIVE TEAM | RESEARCH DATA/NEEDS FINDING | UNIQUE INSIGHTS/ POINT OF VIEW |

MAKING CHOICES → MAKING CHOICES → CREATING CHOICES → MAKING CHOICES →

DIVERGENT OR CONVERGENT

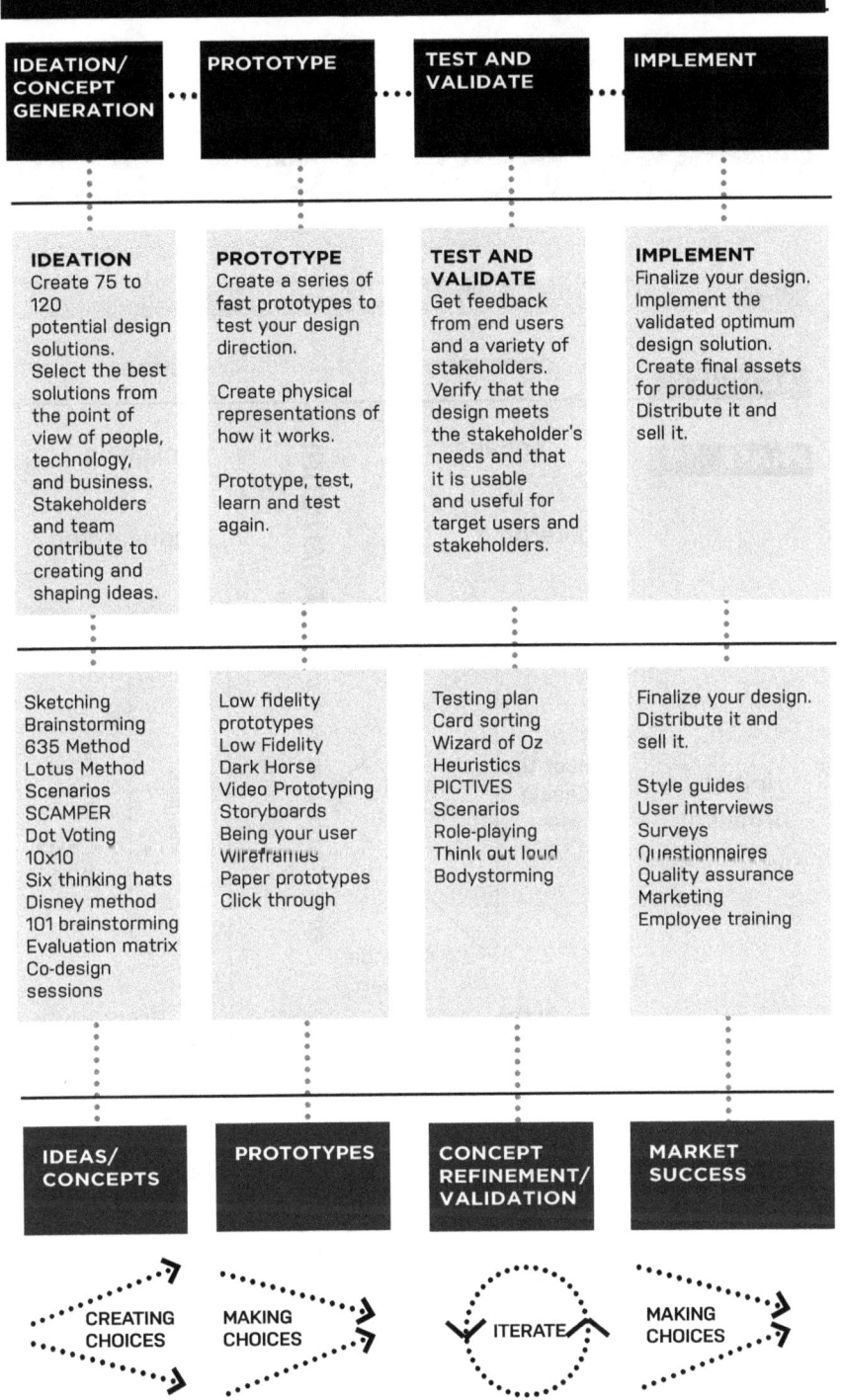

DESIGN PROCESS OVERVIEW

DOUBLE DIAMOND DESIGN PROCESS MODEL

Source: Adapted from process model developed by the British Design Council in 2005

DESIGNING THE RIGHT THING

ACTIVITY	discover		define
PHASE	engage	GROAN ZONE	synthesis
	diverging		converging

- primary research
- select the design team
- cultural immersion
- zone of critical decisions
- clustering
- insights
- point of view
- secondary research
- identify the stakeholders
- How might we questions

initial problem

| KNOWLEDGE | don't know | could be |

IDENTIFYING THE UNMET NEED

DESIGN PROCESS OVERVIEW

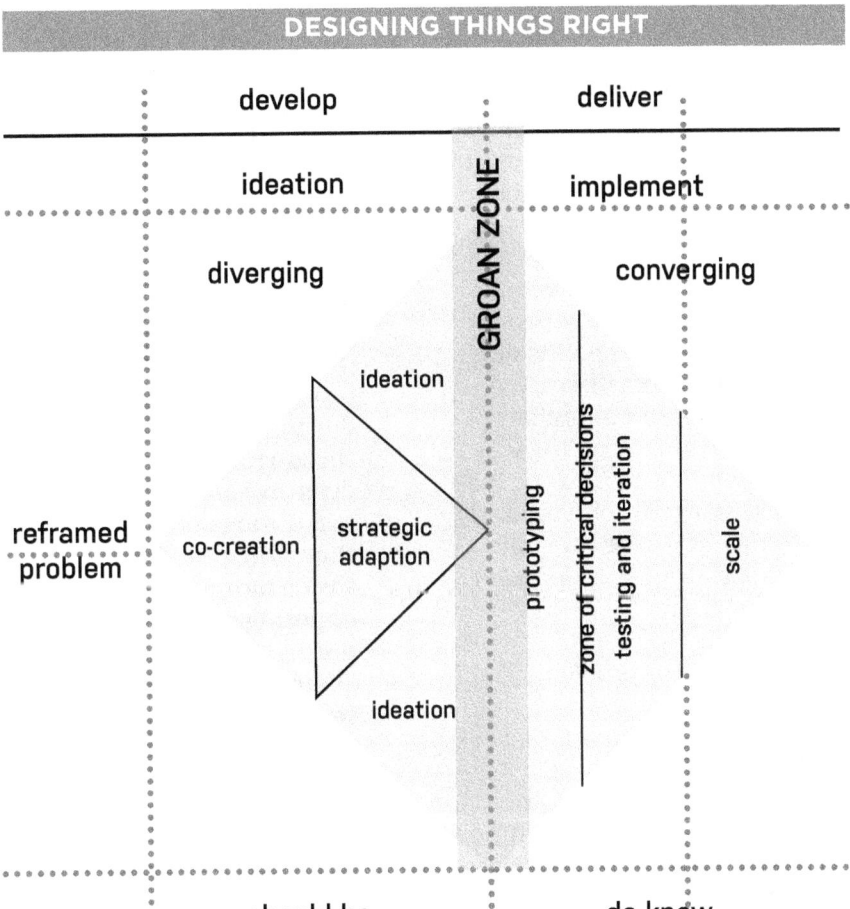

THE GROAN ZONE

> **WHAT**

The groan zone is the place between place between a Divergent state, where many ideas are considered to the convergent state where one direction is found and refined. The groan zone is the transition from to the divergent phase. It is the most difficult and probably the most valuable phase of a design project.

During this phase the different team members will argue their points of view and from discussion and often some conflict a shared understanding will prevail. The groan zone is a necessary part of resolving different perspectives and choosing amongst possible directions.

Challenging problems demand that we push beyond familiar options into new territory in order to solve them. But leaving the familiar behind is uncomfortable and sometimes unpleasant. Solutions reached in the groan zone through a certain level of conflict can be enduring and better solutions.

WHO
This model is described in the Facilitator's Guide to Participatory Decision-Making by Sam Kaner et al (Jossey-Bass, 2nd ed 2007) and further developed by the Art of Hosting community

CHALLENGES
1. Luckner and Nadler (1997) argued that, 'Through involvement in experiences that are beyond one's comfort zone, individuals are forced to move into an area that feels uncomfortable and unfamiliar, the groan zone.
2. Groups experience confusion and frustration as part of their decision-making process. It describes the phase during which members of the group may be insensitive, defensive, ill-tempered, and headstrong and during which they struggle to "understand a wide range of foreign or opposing ideas" (Kaner, 2014, p.19).
3. Disagreement is a divergent state we differ on how to resolve a conflict or solve a problem. Agreement is a convergent state we come together on a resolution or solution.
4. The group experiences feelings close to despair and has a very hard time finding their way forwards in the process.
5. By overcoming these anxious feelings and thoughts of self-doubt while simultaneously sampling success, individuals

move from the groan zone to the growth zone'
6. 'Experience has shown that learning occurs when people are in their stretch zone. Intellectual development and personal growth do not occur if there is no disequilibrium in a person's current thinking or feeling' "Panicucci (2007) (p. 39)
7. Struggling to understand foreign or opposing ideas is not a pleasant experience. Group members can be repetitious, insensitive, defensive, short-tempered!
8. It's uncomfortable there, so we want to hurry through or past it.
9. Tricky, unknown territory brings out the human messiness of conflict, but hurrying through leaves important work undone.
10. It can feel hopeless there.
11. Cultures can avoid conflict due to a preference for interpersonal harmony but this may work against the best ideas rising to the top.

HOW
1. Being in the Groan Zone does NOT mean your group is dysfunctional or that you have reached an impasse. Nor does it mean you are 'failing' as a facilitator. Acknowledge the Groan Zone's existence.
2. It's a usual part of the design process Explain to the team that your are now in the Groan Zone and explain what the groan zone is.
3. Break big issues into smaller parts. Create a list of issues and work through them.
4. Take breaks.
5. Deepen your knowledge of and skill with problem solving strategies and tactics
6. Manage conflict.
7. Staying in the Groan Zone long enough to find innovative solutions.
8. Recognize unproductive comments like "we tried that before."
9. The effort to understand one another's perspectives and build a shared framework of understanding is the defining work of the groan zone.

Being in the Groan Zone does NOT mean your group is dysfunctional or that you have reached an impasse. Nor does it mean you are 'failing' as a facilitator."

Sam Kaner
Participatory Decision-Making

PROTOTYPE TEST ITERATE
How could we make it better?
33. Make your favored ideas physical.
34. Create low-fidelity prototypes from inexpensive available materials.
35. Develop question guides.
36. Develop test plan.
37. Test prototypes with stakeholders.
38. Get feedback from people.
39. Refine the prototypes.
40. Test again.
41. Build in the feedback.
42. Refine again.
43. Continue iteration until design works.
44. When you are confident that your idea works make a prototype that looks and works like a production product.

IMPLEMENT AND DELIVER
Let's make it. Let's sell it.
45. Create your proposed production design.
46. Test and evaluate.
47. Review objectives.
48. Manufacture your first samples.
49. Review first production samples and refine.
50. Launch.
51. Obtain user feedback
52. Conduct field studies.
53. Define the vision for the next product or service.

CHAPTER SUMMARY

The stages of the design thinking process are:

1. Planning
2. Discovery
3. Synthesis
4. Point of view
5. Ideate
6. Prototype and test
7. Implement and deliver.

REVIEW QUESTIONS

1. What are the stages of the design thinking process?
2. Describe the activities in each stage of the design thinking process.
3. What are four methods that can be used in the discovery phase?
4. What are four methods that can be used in the Synthesis phase?
5. What are four methods that can be used in ideation?
6. What are four prototyping methods used in design thinking?
7. What is iteration?
8. What phase of the process is idea brainstorming usually done?
9. What are four things you do during the planning phase?
10. During which phase do you benchmark competitors?
11. What institution developed the double diamond process model?

03
DISCOVERY

DISCOVERY PHASE

WHAT

One of the most important considerations when building a service blueprint is that you use real information relevant to your customers or end users. Organizations very often choose not to connect with their customers to understand their customer's real experience. The methods in this chapter are good methods to collect data to ensure the success of your blueprinting effort. Studies show that greatest single reason for the failure of new products and services is a lack of empathy within the design team of the perspectives of the stakeholders. Over 75% of new product initiatives fail in the market.

During this phase we investigate our users unmet needs and develop a deep understanding of the way they think, what they feel, the behaviors they engage in and the values they hold through engaging them observing and listening to them explain their point of view, their problems, and their underlying needs.

In order to create a design effectively, we need to understand the context that surrounds the end users. We use a variety of research techniques to investigate the user needs and the design context.
By the end of this phase, we will have an overview of user needs, existing services, and their effectiveness and have a foundation to explore many possible design directions. We will investigate the business requirements of the design. We explore user unmet needs through.

1. Workshops
2. Interviews
3. Observation
4. Focus groups
5. Affinity diagrams
6. Discovery methods

DISCOVER
1. Who your users are.
2. Your users' needs and how you're not meeting them.
3. The people you need on your team.
4. What the stakeholder journey or experience looks like.

When you talk, you are only repeating what you know, but when you listen then you learn something new."

Dalai Lama

HOW?
1. Develop empathy for your stakeholders.
2. Develop and implement a research plan.
3. Assume a beginner's mindset.
4. Carry out user research
5. Imagine yourself in that

person's situation.
6. Adopt a beginner's way of thinking. Withhold judgment and preconceived bias.
7. Identify gaps in knowledge.
8. Set aside your beliefs, concerns and personal agenda and try to see things from the stakeholders' points point of view.
9. Question everything. Be curious.
10. Listen.
11. Talk to users to uncover underlying needs.
12. Immerse yourself in your customer's reality.
13. Walk in your user's shoes.
14. Look for your end user's workarounds for their problems.
15. Learn what the stakeholder would do.
16. Immerse yourself in the problem. Walk in your user's shoes, observe what's not being said.
17. Capture your learnings.

OUTPUTS
Outputs of this phase could include:
1. A list of user needs
2. A list of user unmet needs
3. A hierarchy of user needs
4. A plan for the resources required to complete the project.
5. the ability to scope and plan an alpha
6. a decision to progress to next phase
7. Perhaps a low fidelity prototype or several low fidelity prototypes.
8. Four to six personas is an optimum number to cover an organization's customer segments.
9. A list of the most important stakeholders both internally in your organization and externally.
10. A benchmarking of existing or competitive services and a SWOT analysis of these services.
11. A definition of the target audience.

Adapted from Discovery phase Government Service Design Manual, https://www.gov.uk/service-manual/phases/discovery (accessed July 06, 2016).

THE DISCOVERY PROCESS

ASSEMBLE YOUR TEAM
You will need different skills and the team roles and team size may evolve during the different development phases.

Select a diverse cross-disciplinary group of people. Have different disciplines, different genders, ages, cultures, represented for the most successful results. Have some T shaped people. These are people who have more than one area of experience or training such as design and management. They will help your team collaborate productively.

MULTIDISCIPLINARY TEAM
A multidisciplinary team helps you to:
1. Build your service
2. Keep improving it based on user needs
3. Make decisions quickly

TEAM SKILLS
1. Analyze user needs, including accessibility and assisted digital needs, and turn these into user stories
2. Create user stories and prioritize them
3. Manage and report to stakeholders and manage dependencies on other teams
4. Procure services from third parties, if needed
5. Test with real users
6. Find ways of accrediting and

handling data

DEFINE YOUR TARGET AUDIENCE

Creating a projected user models will keep the development team rooted to realistic user requirements and minimizes user frustration with the real product. Having a deep understanding of users can help development team better understand the wants & needs of the targeted customers. This will help the development team relate better to the target user. Understanding user tasks helps in developing design solutions that will ensure that the user expectations are met & avoid design errors and customer frustration. Use research methods such as interviewing, observation, empathy maps and user experience maps to better understand your audience. Market segmentation is basically the division of market into smaller segments. It helps identify potential customers and target them.

TYPES OF SEGMENTATION
1. Behavior segmentation.
2. Benefit segmentation.
3. Psychographic segmentation.
4. Geographic segmentation.
5. Demographic segmentation.

SEGMENTATION QUESTIONS
1. What is your target group's goals emotions, experiences, needs and desires?
2. Information collected from just a few people is unlikely to be representative of the whole range of users.
3. What are the user tasks and activities?
4. How will the user use the product or service to perform a task?
5. What is the context of the user?
6. Where are they? What surrounds them physically and virtually or culturally?
7. How large is your user group?

When defining your target audience consider:
1. Age
2. Gender
3. Occupation
4. Industry
5. Travel
6. Citizenship status
7. Marital state
8. Income
9. Culture
10. Language
11. Religion
12. Location
13. Education
14. Nationality
15. Mobility
16. Migration
17. Mental state
18. Abilities
19. Disabilities
20. Health

SHARE WHAT YOU KNOW
1. In the project kick-off meeting ask every team member to introduce themselves and to describe in 3 minutes what experience they have that may be relevant to the project.
2. The moderator can list areas of knowledge on a whiteboard.
3.

IDENTIFY WHAT YOU NEED TO KNOW

Arrange a project kick-off meeting. Invite your team and important stakeholders. On a whiteboard or flip chart create two lists. Ask each person to introduce themselves and describe what they know or have experienced that may be useful for implementing the project. Brainstorm with your group the areas that are unknown and how that information may be obtained. Formulate a research plan and assign responsibilities, tasks, and deliverables with dates.

UNCOVER NEEDS
1. "What causes the problem?"
2. "What are the impacts of the problem?"
3. "What are possible solutions?"
4. Probe about workarounds How do people adapt their environment to solve problems that they have?
5. Ask what their single biggest obstacle is to achieve what they are trying to achieve How can you help them?
6. Ask what's changing in their world What are the trends?
7. Observe people
8. Can you see problems they have that they perhaps do not even recognize are problems?
9. Ask other stakeholders

DEFINE YOUR GOALS
A goal is the intent or intents of the design process.

1. Write a detailed description of the design problem.
2. Define a list of needs that are connected to the design problem.
3. Make a list of obstacles that need to be overcome to solve the design problem.
4. Make a list of constraints that apply to the problem.
5. Rewrite the problem statement to articulate the above requirements.

> *There is one very important future perspective he [Jonathan Ive] offers though around the increasing complexity and interrelatedness of products and how this requires more effective multidisciplinary working practice to create these products. He explains how they've designed Apple's new donut-like 'Ring' HQ to enable them to create more fully multi-disciplinary design teams, where industrial designers, sound engineers, hardware and software guys, UX people, electronics engineers etc, can all work together throughout the process.*

2017 Soundcloud Interview
Sir Jonathan Ive
Apple VP of Design

SHOP-ALONGS

WHAT

In-store interviews, uncover thoughts, influences, and motivations when consumers are shopping. This research method can be used to investigate the effectiveness of design of packaging, placement, customer experience, and in-aisle marketing. A researcher accompanies a consumer while they browse and shop for items, asking questions as they shop. The interviewer meets the recruited shopper at the door or recruits participants at the door. Shop-alongs are used for collecting real-time, in the moment, and point-of-purchase feedback. A shop-along can be designed for both qualitative or quantitative research. Fifty to one hundred shop-alongs can be used for qualitative analysis. Ten shop-alongs at a local store, could be used for qualitative analysis.

WHEN

Shop-alongs are used In-Store to assess:
1. The purchase decision hierarchy
2. The triggers of the need or desire for the product
3. The behaviors that take place in the store and in the aisle
4. The role of in-store sampling, displays, signs, multi-media promotional efforts, customer service, etc.

WHERE

Retail stores and grocery stores are popular locations for shop-alongs. Locations where a customer may spend 30 minutes naturally shopping are preferred over locations where shopper may usually spend just a few minutes such as a gas station.

HOW

All shop-along projects work a little differently. Each one has their own unique set of circumstances which drive the process and outcomes. However, like many market research projects, they follow a similar process. The process typically involves a kickoff meeting, set up, fieldwork, and then analysis and reporting.

1. Kickoff Meeting

A shop-along starts with a kickoff meeting between the client and the researcher. At this meeting the goals and steps are defined The researcher will then recruit the participants and create the shop-along interview guide design.

2. Recruitment

The demographics and segmentation of the research subjects are defined. This can range to include gender, age, incomes, types of products purchased, stores preferred or many other factors.

3. Choosing Locations

Next the store locations to study are defined.

4. Begin Recruit
The researcher will use a recruitment firm on line panel, or social media to recruit participants to a particular store at a date and time for a 30-minute shop-along. Sometimes researchers recruit at the door as participants walk into the store. Participants are screened to ensure they meet the demographic profile and see if they qualify to participate for the shop-along.

5. Guide Design
The guide contains the script used by the interviewer when they conduct the shop-along. The guide is written to achieve the goals of the shop-along. A good quality guide is important for the success of the research.

6. Conduct the Shop-along
Researchers follow the field guide and record data for each participant and work to promote a natural shopping experience. The interviewer should drop back at non critical times.

7. Analysis and Reporting
Review the data from the shop-longs. Recorded data is transcribed. Comments are broken down. The data is clustered and a hierarchy of importance is determined. The report concludes with a list of insights, conclusions and recommendations.

ANTHROPUMP

WHAT
This method involves the research videotaping one or more participant's activities. The videos are replayed to the participants, and they are asked to explain their behavior.

WHO
Rick Robinson, John Cain, E- Lab Inc.,

WHY
1. Used for collecting data before concept and for evaluating prototypes after concept phases of projects.

CHALLENGES
1. Best conducted by someone who has practice observing human interactions in a space.

HOW
1. People are first captured on video while interacting with products.
2. The participants are then asked to watch the tapes while researchers question them about what they see, how they felt, etc. Research subjects analyze their actions and experiences.
3. The company invites people who have been captured on video to watch their tapes as researchers pose questions about what's happening.
4. Create videotapes and examines these follow-up sessions, analyzing research subjects analyzing themselves.

BEHAVIORAL MAP

WHAT
Behavioral mapping is a method used to record and analyze human activities in a location. This method is used to document what participants are doing and time spent at locations and traveling. Behavioral maps can be created based on a person or space.

WHO
Ernest Becker 1962

WHY
1. This method helps develop an understanding of space layouts, interactions, experiences, and behaviors.
2. Helps understand way- finding.
3. Helps optimize the use of space.
4. A limitation of this method is that motivations remain unknown.
5. Use when you want to develop more efficient or effective use of space in retail environments, exhibits, architecture and interior design.

HOW
1. Identify the users.
2. Ask what is the purpose of the space?
3. Consider what behaviors are meaningful.
4. Consider different personas.
5. Participants can be asked to map their use of a space on a floor plan and can be asked to reveal their motivations.
6. Can use shadowing or video ethnographic techniques.
7. Create behavioral map.
8. Analyze behavioral map

9. Reorganize space based on insights.

RESOURCES
A map of the space.
Video camera
Digital still camera
Notebook
Pens

BENCHMARKING

WHAT
Benchmarking is a method for organizations to compare their products, services or customer experiences with other industry products, services and experiences to identify the best practices.

WHO
Robert Camp Xerox, 1989 Benchmarking: the search for industry best practices that lead to superior performance.

WHY
1. A tool to identify, and implement the best practices.
2. The practice of measuring your performance against best competitors.

CHALLENGES
1. Can be expensive
2. Organizations often think their companies were performing above the average for the industry when they are not.

HOW
1. Identify what your objective.
2. Identify potential partners
3. Identify similar industries and organizations.
4. Identify organizations that are leaders.
5. Identify data sources
6. Identify the products or organizations to be benchmarked
7. Select the benchmarking factors to measure.
8. Undertake benchmarking
9. Research the "best practice" organizations
10. Analyze the outcomes
11. Target future performance
12. Adjust goal
13. Modify your own product or service to conform with best practices identified in the benchmarking process.

RESOURCES
Post-it-notes
Pens
Dry-erase markers
White-board
Paper

BENEFITS MAP

WHAT
The benefits map is a simple tool that helps your team decide what will give you the best return on investment for time invested.

WHY
1. Aids communication and discussion within the organization.
2. It is human nature to do tasks which are not most urgent first.
3. To gain competitive advantage,
4. Helps build competitive strategy
5. Helps build communication strategy
6. Helps manage time effectively

DISCOVERY PHASE

CHALLENGES
Can be subjective

HOW
1. Moderator draws axes on whiteboard or flip chart.
2. Worthwhile activity at the start of a project.
3. Map individual tasks.
4. Interpret the map.
5. Create strategy.
6. Tasks which have high benefit with low investment may be given priority.

BOUNDARY SHIFTING

WHAT
Boundary shifting involves identifying features or ideas outside the boundary of the system related to the defined problem and applying to them to the problem being addressed.

WHY
It is fast and inexpensive.

HOW
1. Define the problem.
2. Research outside systems that may have related ideas or problems to the defined problem.
3. Identify ideas or solutions outside the problem system.
4. Apply the outside idea or solution to the problem being addressed.

RESOURCES
1. Pen
2. Paper
3. White-board
4. Dry-erase markers

CAMERA JOURNAL

WHAT
The research subjects record their activities with a camera and notes. The researcher reviews the images and discusses them with the participants.

WHY
1. Helps develop empathy for the participants.
2. Participants are involved in the research process.
3. Helps establish rapport with participants.
4. May reveal aspects of life that are seldom seen by outsiders.

CHALLENGES
1. Should obtain informed consent.
2. Be sensitive to vulnerable people.
3. May be a relatively expensive research method.
4. May be time-consuming.
5. Best used with other methods.
6. Technology may be unreliable.
7. The method may be unpredictable'.
8. Has to be carefully analyzed

HOW
1. Define subject of study
2. Define participants
3. Gather data images and insight statements.
4. Analyze data.
5. Identify insights
6. Rank insights
7. Produce criteria for concept generation from insights.
8. Generate concepts to meet needs of users.

RESOURCES
Cameras
Voice recorder

Video camera
Notepad computer
Pens

OPEN CARD SORT

WHAT
This is a method for discovering the relationships of a list of items. Participants are asked to arrange individual, unsorted items into groups. For an open card sort, the user defines the groups rather than the researcher.

CARD SORTING IS APPLIED WHEN:
9. When there is a large number of items.
10. The items are similar and difficult to organize into categories.
11. Users may have different perceptions related to organizing the items.

WHO
Jastrow 1886
Nielsen & Sano 1995

WHY
1. It is a simple method using index cards,
2. Used to provide insights for interface design.

CHALLENGES
1. Ask participants to fill out a second card if they feel it belongs in two groups.
2. There are a number of online card sorting tools available.

HOW

1. Recruit between 5 and 15 participants representative of your user group.
2. Provide a small deck of cards.
3. Provide clear instructions. Ask your participants to arrange the cards in ways that make sense to them. One hundred cards take about 1 hour to sort.
4. The user sorts labeled cards into groups by that they define themselves.
5. The user can generate more card labels.
6. If users do not understand a card ask them to exclude it. Ask participants for their rationale for any dual placements of cards.
7. Analyze the piles of cards and create a list of insights derived from the card sort.
8. Analyze the data.

CLOSED CARD SORT

WHAT
This is a method for understanding the relationships of a number of pieces of data. Participants asked to arrange individual, unsorted items into groups. A closed sort involves the cards being sorted into groups where the group headings may be defined by the researcher.

Card sorting is applied when:
1. When there is a large number of pieces of data.
2. The individual pieces of data are similar.
3. Participants have different perceptions of the data.

WHO
Jastrow 1886
Nielsen & Sano 1995

WHY
1. It is a simple method using index cards,
2. Used to provide insights for interface design.

HOW
1. Recruit 15 to 20 participants representative of your user group.
2. Provide a deck of cards using words and or images relevant to your concept.
3. Provide clear instructions. Ask your participants to arrange the cards in ways that make sense to them. 100 cards takes about 1 hour to sort.
4. The user sorts labeled cards into groups by under header cards defined by the researcher.
5. The user can generate more card labels.
6. If users do not understand a card ask them to exclude it. Ask participants for their rationale for any dual placements of cards.
7. Discuss why the cards are placed in a particular pile yields insight into user perceptions.
8. Analyze the data. Create a hierarchy for the information
9. Use postcards or post-it notes.

RESOURCES
Post cards
Pens
Post-it-notes
Laptop computer
A table

CONVERSATION CARDS

WHAT
Cards used for initiating conversation in a contextual interview and to help subjects explore.

WHO
Originator unknown. Google Ngram indicates the term first appeared around 1801 in England for a collection of "Moral and Religious Anecdotes particularly adapted for the entertainment and instruction of young persons, and to support instead of destroying serious conversation."

WHY
1. Questions are the springboard for conversations.
2. Can be used to initiate sensitive conversations.

CHALLENGES
1. How will data from the cards be used?
2. How will cards be evaluated?
3. How many cards are necessary to be representative?
4. What are potential problems relating card engagement
5. Use one unit of information per question.

HOW
1. Decide on the goals for research.
2. Formulate about 10 questions related to topic
3. Create the cards.
4. Recruit the subjects.
5. Undertake pre-interview with sample subject to test.
6. Use release form if required.

7. Carry light equipment.
8. Record answers verbatim.
9. Communicate the purpose and length of the interview.
10. Select location. It should not be too noisy or have other distracting influences
11. Work through the cards.
12. Video or record the sessions for later review.
13. Analyze
14. Create Insights

RESOURCES
Conversation Cards.
Notebook
Video Camera
Pens
Interview plan or structure
Questions, tasks and discussion items

Interview cards

CULTURAL INVENTORY

WHAT
It is a survey focused on the cultural assets of a location or organization.

WHO
Julian Haynes Steward may have been the first to use the term in 1947.

WHY
1. Can be used in strategic planning
2. Can be used to solve problems.

CHALLENGES
Requires time and resources

HOW
1. Create your team
2. Collect existing research
3. Review existing research and identify gaps
4. Host a meeting of stakeholders
5. Promote the meeting
6. Ask open-ended questions about the culture and heritage
7. Set a time limit of 2 hours for the meeting.
8. Plan the collection phase
9. Compile inventory. This can be in the form of a website
10. Distribute the inventory and obtain feedback.

RESOURCES
Diary
Notebooks
Pens
Post-it notes
Voice recorder
Postcards
Digital Camera

CULTURAL PROBES

WHAT
A cultural probe is a method of collecting information about people, their context, and their culture. The aim of this method is to record events, behaviors, and interactions in their context. This method involves the participants to record and collect the data themselves.

WHO
Bill Gaver Royal College of Art London 1969

WHY
1. This is a useful method when the participants that are being studied are hard to reach for

example if they are traveling.
2. It is a useful technique if the activities being studied take place over an extended period or at irregular intervals.
3. The information collected can be used to build personas.

CHALLENGES
It is important with this method to select the participants carefully and give them support during the study.

HOW
1. Define the objective of your study.
2. Recruit your participants.
3. Brief the participants.
4. Supply participants with kit. The items in the kit are selected to collect the type of information you want to gather and can include items such as notebooks, diary, camera, voice recorder or postcards.
5. You can use an affinity diagram to analyze the data collected.

DAY EXPERIENCE METHOD

WHAT
The method requires participants to record answers to questions during a day. The person's mobile phone is used to prompt them The participants use a notebook, a camera or a voice recorder to answer your questions. The interviews are followed by a focus group.

WHO
Intille 2003

WHY
1. The participants are co-researchers.
2. Reduces the influence of the researcher on the participant when compared to methods such as interviews or direct observation.

CHALLENGES
1. Cost of devices.
2. This method should be used with other methods.

HOW
1. Conduct a preliminary survey to focus the method on preferred questions.
2. Recruit participants.
3. The experience sampling takes place over one day.
4. The participants are asked to provide answers to questions at irregular intervals when promoted by a SMS message via the participant's mobile phone.
5. The interval can be 60 to 90-minutes.
6. The participant can record the activity with a camera, notebook or voice recorder.
7. Soon after the day organize a focus group with the participants.
8. The participants describe their day using the recorded material.

RESOURCES
Mobile phone
Automated SMS messaging
Notebook
Camera
Software

*Day Experience Resource Kit
Matthew Riddle,*

DAY IN THE LIFE

WHAT
A study in which the designer observes the participant in the location and context of their usual activities, observing and recording events to understand the activities from the participant's point of view. Mapping a 'Day in the Life' as a storyboard can provide a focus for discussion.

WHO
Alex Bavelas 1944

WHY
1. This method informs the design process by observation of real activities and behaviors.
2. This method provides insights with relatively little cost and time.

CHALLENGES
1. Choose the participants carefully
2. Document everything. Something that seems insignificant may become significant later.

HOW
1. Define activities to study
2. Recruit participants
3. Prepare
4. Observe subjects in context.
5. Capture data,
6. Create storyboard with text and timeline.
7. Analyze data
8. Create insights.
9. Identify issues
10. Identify needs
11. Add new/more requirements to concept development

DOT VOTING

WHAT
Dot voting is a way of efficiently selecting from a large number of ideas the preferred ideas to carry forward in the design process.

WHY
It is a method of selecting a favored idea by collective rather than individual judgment. It is a fast method that allows a design to progress. It leverages the strengths of diverse team member viewpoints and experiences.

CHALLENGES
1. The assessment is subjective.
2. Groupthink
3. Not enough good ideas
4. Inhibition
5. Lack of critical thinking

RESOURCES
Large wall
Adhesive dots

HOW
1. Gather your team of between four and twelve participants.
2. Brainstorm ideas, for example, ask each team member to generate between ten and thirty ideas as sketches.
3. Each idea should be presented on one post-it-note or page.
4. Each designer should quickly explain each idea to the group before the group votes.
5. Spread the ideas on a wall or table.
6. Ask the team to vote on their two or three favorite ideas and total the votes. You can use sticky

dots or colored pins to indicate a vote or a moderator can tally the scores.
7. Rearrange the ideas ranked from most dots to least.
8. Refine the preferred ideas.

DIARY STUDY

WHAT
This method involves participants recording particular events, feelings or interactions, in a diary supplied by the researcher. User Diaries help provide insight into behavior. Participants record their behavior and thoughts. Diaries can uncover behaviour that may not be articulated in an interview or readily visible to outsiders.

WHO
Gordon Allport, may have been the first to describe diary studies in 1942.

WHY
1. Can capture data that is difficult to capture using other methods.
2. Useful when you wish to gather information and minimize your influence on research subjects.
3. When the process or event you're exploring takes place over a long period.

CHALLENGES
1. Process can be expensive and time-consuming.
2. Needs participant monitoring.
3. It is difficult to get materials back.

HOW
1. A diary can be kept over a period of one week or longer.
2. Define focus for the study.
3. Recruit participants carefully.
4. Decide method: preprinted, diary notebook or online.
5. Prepare diary packs. Can be preprinted sheets or blank twenty-page notebooks with prepared questions or online web-based diary.
6. Brief participants.
7. Distribute diaries directly or by mail.
8. Conduct study. Keep in touch with participants.
9. Conduct debrief interview.
10. Look for insights.

RESOURCES
Diary
Preprinted diary sheets
Online diary
Pens
Disposable cameras
Digital camera
Self-addressed envelopes

BIASES

We all have unconscious biases. These biases can reduce the effectiveness of our decision-making in design thinking. Understanding our own biases can help us overcome them. Understanding the biases of others can help us improve the user experience and help us better understand team dynamics and diversity.

COGNITIVE DISSONANCE

Cognitive dissonance is the stress experienced by a person who simultaneously holds contradictory beliefs, ideas, or values.

Leon Festinger proposed in 1957 that people strive for internal psychological consistency. A person is motivated to reduce the cognitive inconsistency by changing parts of the cognition to justify the behavior, by adding new parts, or by avoiding contradictory information that are likely to increase the cognitive dissonance.

FALSE CAUSALITY

A bias that involves concluding that since one event followed another in time, the first must have caused the second. False causality is jumping to a conclusion of a causal relationship without supporting evidence.

ACTION BIAS

When faced with an ambiguous problem we sometimes prefer to do something, if it is counterproductive, even when doing nothing is the best course of action.

AMBIGUITY BIAS

If an outcome is risky and unknown, there is a tendency to stick to what is already known and stay with what you've done previously.

STRATEGIC MISREPRESENTATION

This is understating the costs and overstating the likely benefits in order to get a project approved.

GROUPTHINK

Group-think is a type of bias that occurs within a group in which the desire for harmony in the group results in dysfunctional decision-making. Group members try to minimize conflict and reach a consensus decision without critical evaluation, and by isolating themselves from other points of view.

INNOVATION BIAS

Novelty and 'newness' are seen as good, regardless of potential negative impacts.

ANCHORING BIAS

This type of bias involves being influenced by information that is already known or that has just been shown.

STATUS-QUO BIAS

This bias involves favoring a current situation or status quo and maintaining it.. This bias makes us reduce risk and prefer what is familiar and can stand in the way of innovation.

FRAMING BIAS

Being influenced by the way in which information is presented rather than the information itself. People react to a particular choice in different ways depending on how it is presented. An audience tends to avoid risk when a positive frame is presented but seek risks when a negative frame is presented.

CONFLICTS OF INTEREST
A conflict of interest is when a person or organization has conflicting financial, personal or other interests which could corrupt and lead to improper actions.

FUNDING BIAS
Funding bias refers to the tendency of a study to support the interests of the financial sponsor.
Source: Jono Hey

FUNCTIONAL FIXEDNESS
Functional fixedness limits a person to using an object only in the way it's traditionally used.

NARRATIVE FALLACY
Our brains love stories. Narrative. When something is framed as a story, it's memorable, convincing, and easy to understand. It is easy to draw false conclusions.

SURVIVOR BIAS
"Survivorship bias refers to our tendency to focus on the winners in a particular area and try to learn from them while completely forgetting about the losers who are employing the same strategy."

THE IKEA EFFECT
The IKEA effect is a cognitive bias in which consumers place a disproportionately high value on products they partially created.

RESEARCH PLAN

WHAT
The research plan gives a design team and stakeholders the opportunity to discuss proposed research, stating its importance, why and how it will be conducted and costs. It is best to keep it as short and concise as possible.

WHY
A well-structured research plan

1. A communication tool.
2. Provides a clear focus.
3. Creates team alignment
4. Provides a forum to ask questions.
5. Creates an expectation of knowledge gained.
6. Will improve your final design.

HOW
Sections to include

1. Executive summary
2. Problem statement
3. State concisely the goals of the proposed research.
4. Why is the work important
5. What has already been done
6. User profile
7. Stakeholders and their needs
8. Methodology
9. Research questions [5]
10. Number of participants
11. Length of session
12. Where will the research take place?
13. Roles and responsibilities
14. Test artifacts
15. Participant incentive
16. Scenarios
17. Evaluation methods
18. Test environment and equipment
19. Project timeline

20. Deliverables
21. Where supporting information can be found

Sample research activities
1. Preparation for a single project: ten hours
2. Recruiting and scheduling: two to three hours per person
3. Contextual inquiry/task analysis: five hours per person
4. Focus groups: three hours per group
5. Usability tests: three hours per participant
6. Analyzing contextual inquiry/task analysis: five hours per person
7. Analyzing focus group results: four hours per group
8. Analyzing usability tests: two hours per person
9. Preparing a report for email delivery: twelve hours
10. Preparing a one-hour presentation: six hours

Sample timeline
Pilot Testing date: November 25th, 2017 6PM-7PM Pilot User

Testing date: November 30th, 2017

8AM - 9AM Setup testing area
9AM - 10AM Participant 1
10:15AM - 11:15 Participant 2
11:15AM - 12:30 Lunch
12:30PM - 1:30 Participant 3
1:45PM - 2:45 Participant 4
3:00PM - 4:00PM Participant 5
4:15PM - 5:15
Debriefing and wrap-up
Presentation to Client: December 14th 6:00PM-8:00PM
Formal Report Submitted: April 28th

SAMPLE ONE-PAGE RESEARCH PLAN
Title
ABC Laptop Data-Entry Usability Test
By John Smith-Doe, Usability

Stakeholders
Wanda Answer (PM),
Sam Doe (Lead Engineer)

Background
Since January 2009, when the ABC laptop was introduced to the world, particularly after its market release, journalists, bloggers, industry experts, other stakeholders and customers have privately and publicly expressed negative opinions about the ABC laptop's keyboard. These views suggest that the keyboard is hard to use and that it imposes a poor experience on customers. Some have claimed this as the main reason why the ABC laptop will not succeed among business users. Over the years, several improvements have been made to keyboard design to no avail.

Goals
Identify the strengths and weaknesses of data entry on the ABC laptop, and provide opportunities for improvement.

Research Questions
1. How do people enter data on the ABC laptop?
2. What is the learning curve of new ABC laptop users when they enter data?
3. What are the most common errors users make when entering data?

Methodology
A usability study will be held in our lab with 20 participants. Each participant session will last 60-minutes and will include a

DISCOVERY PHASE 61

short briefing, an interview, a task performance with an ABC laptop and a debriefing. Among the tasks: enter an email subject heading, compose a long email, check news updates on Washington Post's's website, create a calendar event and more.

Participants
These are the primary characteristics of the study participants:
- Business user
- Age 22 to 55,
- Never used an ABC Phone,
- Expressed interest in learning more about or purchasing an ABC laptop,
- Uses the Web at least 10 hours a week.
- [Link to a draft screener]

Schedule
Recruiting: begins October 12
Study day: October 22
Results delivery: November 2

Attachments
Script

Source: Adapted from smashingmagazine.com

EMOTION CARDS

WHAT

Emotion cards are a field method of analyzing and quantifying people's emotional response to a design. The method classifies emotions into sets of emotions which each can be associated with a specific recognizable facial expression.

The emotion card tool consists of sixteen cartoon-like faces, half male, and half female, each representing distinct emotions. Each face describes a combination of two emotion dimensions, pleasure, and arousal. Based on these dimensions, the emotion cards can be divided into four quadrants: Calm-Pleasant, Calm-Unpleasant, Excited-Pleasant, and Excited-Unpleasant.

WHO
Bradley 1994

WHY
1. It is an inexpensive method.
2. The results are easy to analyze.
3. Emotional responses are subtle and difficult to measure.
4. Emotion cards is a cross-cultural tool.
5. Facial emotions are typically universally recognized

CHALLENGES
1. Emotions of male and female faces are interpreted differently.
2. Sometimes users want to mark

more than one picture to express a more complex emotional response.

HOW
1. Decide the goal of the study.
2. Recruit the participants.
3. Brief the participants.
4. When each interaction is complete the researcher asks the participant to select one of a number of cards that shows facial expressions that they associate with the interaction.

RESOURCES
Emotion cards
Notebook
Pens
Video camera
Release forms
Interview plan or structure
Questions, tasks and discussion items
Emotion cards

FIVE WHYS

WHAT
Five whys is an iterative question method used to discover the underlying cause of a problem. For every effect, there is a root cause. The primary goal of the technique is to determine the underlying cause of a problem by repeating the question "Why?"

WHO
The technique was originally developed by Sachichi Toyoda Sakichi Toyoda was a Japanese inventor and industrialist. He was born in Kosai, Shizuoka. The son of a poor carpenter, Toyoda is referred to as the "King of Japanese Inventors". He was the founder of the Toyota Motor company. The method is still an important part of Toyota training, culture and success.

Sakichi Toyoda -

WHY
When we fix the root cause the problem does not reoccur

HOW
1. Five whys could be taken further to a sixth, seventh, or higher level, but five is generally sufficient to get to a root cause.
2. Gather a team and develop the problem statement in agreement
3. Establish the time and place that the problem is occurring
4. Ask the first "why" of the team: why is this problem taking place?
5. Ask four more successive "whys," repeating the process
6. You will have identified the root cause when asking "why" yields no further useful information.
7. Discuss the last answers and settle on the most likely systemic cause.
8. Fix the root problem

FLY-ON-THE-WALL

WHAT
Observation method where the observer remains as unobtrusive as possible and observes and collects data relevant to a research study in context with no interaction with the participants being observed. The name derived from the documentary film technique of the same name.

DISCOVERY PHASE

DESCRIPTIVE QUESTION MATRIX
Spradley, J. 1980. Participant observation. New York Holt, Rinehart & Winston

	SPACE	OBJECT	ACT	ACTIVITY
SPACE The physical place or places	Can you describe in detail all the places?	What are all the ways space is organized by objects?	What are all the ways that space are organized by actions?	What are all the ways space is organized by activities?
OBJECT The physical things that are present	Where are objects located?	Can you describe in detail all the objects?	What are all the ways objects are used in acts?	What are all the ways objects are used in activities?
ACT Single actions that people do	What are all the places acts occur?	What are all the ways acts incorporate objects?	Can you describe in detail all the acts?	What are all the ways that acts are involved in activities?
ACTIVITY A set of related acts people do	What are all the places activities occur?	What are all the ways activities incorporate objects?	What are all the ways activities incorporate acts?	Can you describe in detail all the activities?
EVENT A set of related activities that people carry out	What are all the places events occur?	What are all the ways events incorporate objects?	What are all the ways events incorporate acts?	What are all the ways events incorporate activities?
TIME The sequencing that takes place over time	Where do time periods occur?	What are all the ways time affects objects?	How do acts fall into time periods?	How do activities fall into time periods?
ACTOR The people involved	Where do actors place themselves?	What are all the ways actors use objects?	How are actors involved in acts?	How are actors involved in activities?
GOAL The things people are trying to accomplish	Where are goals sought and achieved?	What are all the ways goals involve use of objects?	What are all the ways goals involve acts?	What activities are goal seeking or linked to goals?
FEELINGS The emotions felt and expressed	Where do the various feeling states occur?	What feelings lead to the use of what objects?	What are all the ways feelings affect acts?	What are all the ways feelings affect activities?

DESCRIPTIVE QUESTION MATRIX

Spradley, J. 1980. Participant observation. New York Holt, Rinehart & Winston

EVENT	TIME	ACTOR	GOAL	FEELINGS
What are all the ways space is organized by events?	What spatial changes occur over time?	What are all the ways space is used by actors?	What are all the ways space is related to goals?	What places are associated with feelings?
What are all the ways objects are used in events?	What are all the ways objects are used in activities?	What are all the ways objects are used by actors?	How are objects used in seeking goals?	What are all the ways objects evoke feelings?
What are all the ways that acts are involved in events?	How do acts vary at different times?	What are all the ways acts incorporate actors?	What are all the ways acts involve goals?	How do acts involve feelings?
What are all the ways that activities are involved in events?	How do activities vary at different times?	What are all the ways activities incorporate actors?	What are all the ways activities involve goals?	How do activities involve feelings?
Can you describe in detail all the events?	How do events occur over time? Is there an order of events?	What are all the ways events incorporate actors?	What are all the ways events involve goals?	How do events involve feelings?
How do events fall into time periods?	Can you describe in detail all the time periods?	When are all the times actors are "on stage"?	How are goals related to time periods?	When are feelings evoked?
How are actors involved in events?	How do actors change over time or at different times?	Can you describe in detail all the actors?	Which actors are linked to which goals?	What are the feelings experienced by actors?
What are all the ways goals involve events?	Which goals are scheduled for which times?	How do the various goals affect the various actors?	Can you describe in detail all the goals?	What are all the ways goals evoke feelings?
What are all the ways feelings affect events?	How are feelings related to various time periods?	What are all the ways feelings involve actors?	What are the ways feelings influence goals?	Can you describe in detail all the feelings?

ACTIVITY MAP

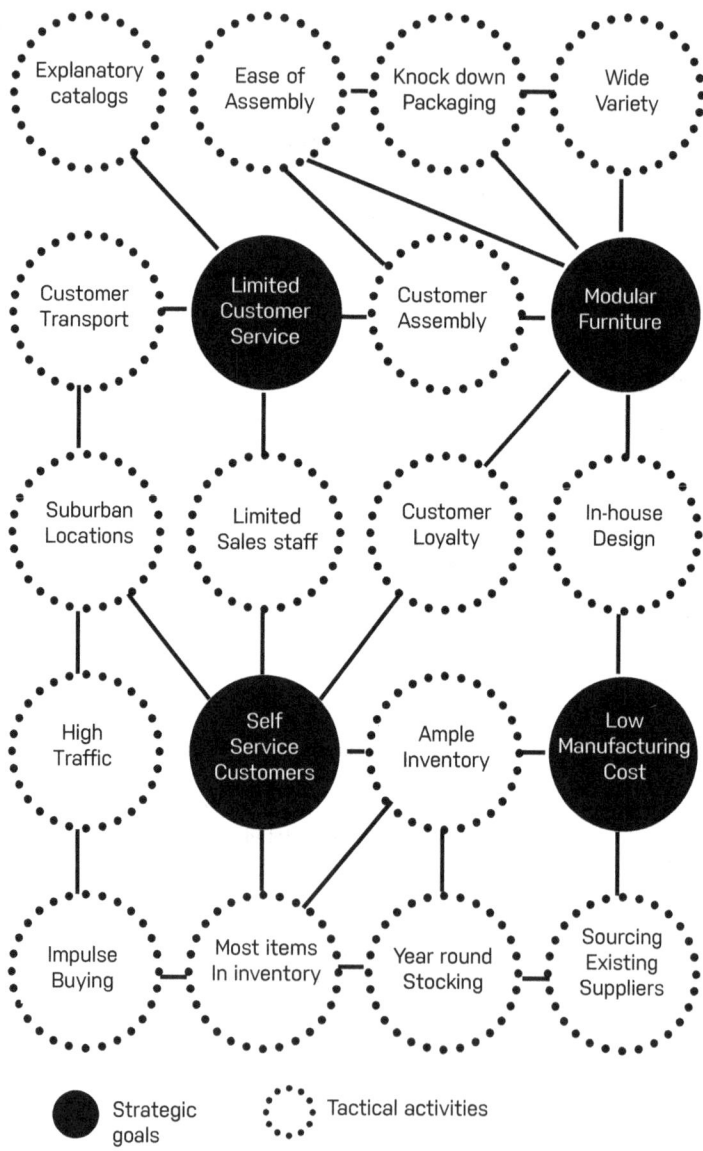

Source: Activity map for IKEA (after Porter)

WHO
Alex Bavelas 1944
Lucy Vernile, Robert A. Monteiro 1991

WHY
1. Low cost
2. No setup necessary
3. Can observe a large number of participants.
4. Objective observations
5. Compared to focus groups, setup, data collection, and processing are much faster.

CHALLENGES
1. No interaction by the observer.
2. Observer cannot delve deeper during a session.
3. No interruption allowed
4. Observer cannot obtain details on customer comments during a session

HOW
1. Define activity to study
2. Select participants thoughtfully
3. Choose a context for the observation
4. Carefully observe the interaction or experience. This is best done by members of your design team.
5. It is important to influence the participants as little as possible by your presence.
6. Observe but do not interact with participants while observing them in context.
7. Capture Data
8. Identify issues
9. Identify needs
10. Create design solutions based on observed and experienced human needs.

FOCUS GROUPS

WHAT
Focus groups are discussions usually with 6 to 12 participants led by a moderator. Focus groups are used during the the design of products, services and experiences to get feedback from people. They are often conducted in the evening and take on average two hours. 8 to 12 questions are commonly explored in a discussion.

> **The purpose of focus groups is not to infer, but to understand, not to generalize but to determine a range, not to make statements about the population but to provide insights about how people perceive a situation."**

Richard A. Krueger

WHO
Robert K. Merton 1940 Bureau of Applied Social Research.

WHY
1. Low cost per participant compared to other research methods.
2. Easier than some other methods to manage

CHALLENGES
1. Removes participants from their context.
2. Requires a skilled moderator.
3. Focus group study results may not be generalizable.
4. Focus group participants can influence each other.

DISCOVERY PHASE 67

HOW
1. Select a good moderator.
2. Prepare a screening questionnaire.
3. Decide incentives for participants.
4. Select facility.
5. Recruit participants. Invite participants to your session well in advance and get firm commitments to attend. Remind participants the date of the event.
6. Participants should sit around a large table. Follow discussion guide.
7. Describe rules. Provide refreshments.
8. First question should encourage talking and participation.
9. The moderator manages responses and asks important questions
10. Moderator collects forms and debriefs focus group.
11. Analyze results while still fresh.
12. Summarize key points.
13. Run additional focus groups to deepen analysis.

IDEATION DECISION MATRIX

WHAT
A process to lead the group to consensus on a specific solution Ideas are listed and each member ranks the ideas: 1=best, 2=2nd best, ...n=least favorite. Rankings are collated, added and the top 3-5 LOWEST totals are used in the next step.

WHEN?
1. You have time between ideation and synthesis phases.
2. You have used a computer or email so circulation of the brainstorm list is fast and easy

CHALLENGES
1. Should obtain informed consent.
2. May not be ideal for research among vulnerable people.
3. May be a relatively expensive research method.
4. May be time-consuming.
5. Best used with other methods.
6. Technology may be unreliable.
7. Method may be unpredictable.
8. Has to be carefully analyzed.

HOW
1. Define subject of study
2. Define participants
3. Gather data images and insight statements.
4. Analyze data.
5. Identify insights
6. Rank insights
7. Produce criteria for concept generation from insights.
8. Generate concepts to meet needs of users.

WHY
1. Effective (members use measures to reach agreement)
2. Time-sensitive (agreement is quick)
3. Easy (one form, 4 steps)
4. Everyone's evaluation is valid
5. Math is used to consolidate
6. Highest Result = Consensus

HOW
1. Each person puts a value from 5(high) to 1(low) on each ideas for their effectiveness and then for feasibility.
2. Total values by criteria.
3. Multiply total effectiveness by total feasibility.
4. Highest product is your chosen solution.

BENCHMARKING MATRIX FOR PRODUCT DESIGN

Criteria	A	B	C	D	E	F	G	H	I
Usability	1	2	3	1	4	1	1	2	3
Speed to market	2	1	1	2	2	4	2	1	4
Brand compatibility	2	4	0	2	2	4	0	4	4
Roi	2	3	1	1	4	1	1	3	3
Fits strategy	1	1	1	4	0	3	1	2	2
Aesthetic appeal	2	4	0	2	2	4	0	4	4
Differentiation	2	2	2	0	1	1	3	3	0
Tooling cost	2	2	1	1	1	2	0	4	3
Fits distribution	2	2	3	1	2	1	4	0	3
Uses our factory	3	3	5	3	0	3	2	1	3
Fits trends	1	3	2	2	1	3	4	3	2
Total	21	26	23	18	20	23	21	24	29

BENEFITS MAP

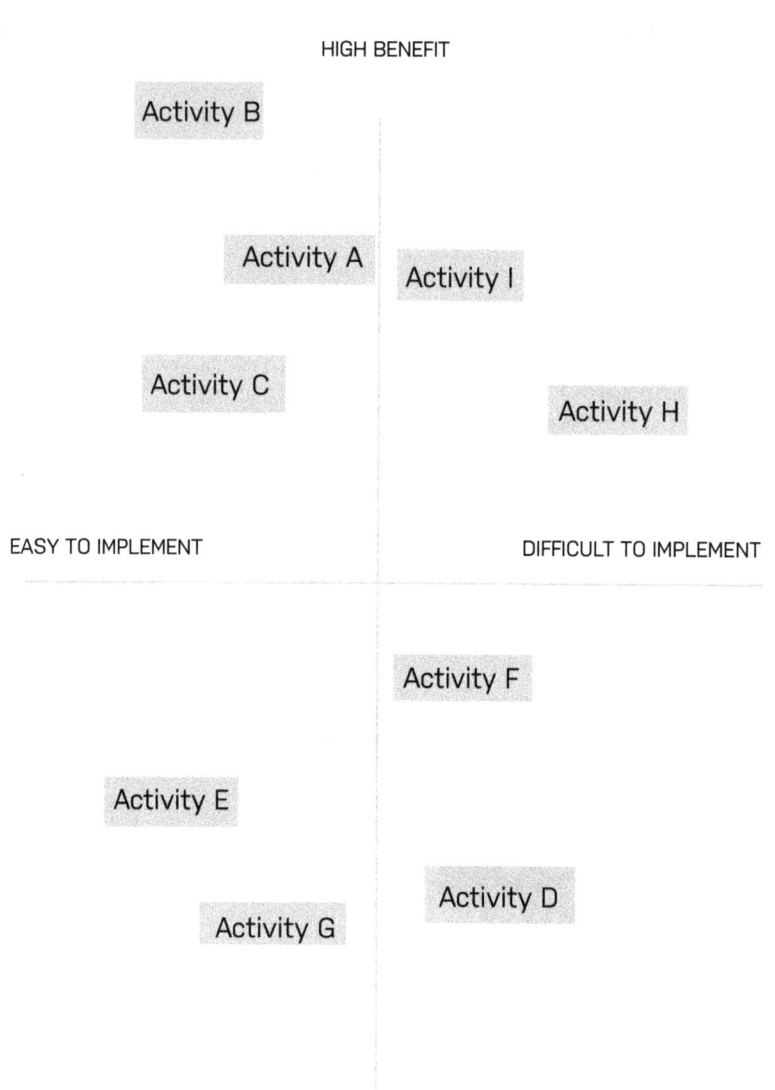

INTERVIEWS

PLANNING INTERVIEWS

WHY
1. More in-depth information than other methods.
2. Uncover tacit or day to day knowledge not available from secondary sources.
3. Low costs.
4. Understand the end user point of view.

CHALLENGES
1. Doesn't yield quantitative information.
2. Transcribing interviews takes time.
3. Some subjects may not want to be recorded.
4. Interviews are best conducted in situ or in the context of use of a design.
5. Both the interviewer and interviewee have some biases.

PLANNING
1. What information do you need to uncover?
2. Is interviewing the best way to uncover the information that you need?
3. Who should you interview?
4. How will you identify the interviewees?
5. What is their experience and diversity of experience?
6. Where should the interviews be conducted?
7. When should you conduct the interviews?
8. How should you conduct the interviews?
9. List your goals.
10. How will the information be used?
11. How will you communicate the findings?
12. What is your primary question?
13. How many people should you interview?
14. How long will the interviews take and how long will it take to transcribe the interviews?
15. It takes 4 to 6 hours to transcribe one recorded hour of an interview.
16. Who is your audience and what method will you use to communicate with them?
17. What is the timeline? Create a timeline that addresses the following: preliminary research, locating interviewees, conducting interviews, transcribing the interviews, analyzing the transcripts, and formulating the finalized product of your project. Formulate rough deadlines to keep yourself on track.
18. Who will conduct the interviews?
19. Do the interviewers need to be trained?
20. Be aware of and minimize interviewer bias interviewees may respond differently to different interviewers based upon differences in interview style, age, race, class, gender, or culture.
21. What language will interviews be conducted in?
22. Is interpretation needed during the interview?
23. What tools or equipment will you need?
24. You will need tape, video, or digital recorders to record the interviews. A computer is needed transcribe the interview.
25. Who will transcribe the interviews?
26. What resources, people and money, will be needed?
27. How will you address confidentiality? Will you need a non disclosure agreement?
28. How will the data be analyzed?

29. Who will write the report or communicate the findings? materials?

CONDUCTING THE INTERVIEW
1. Create a list of people to interview.
2. Contact them and set up a time to meet.
3. Allow 2 hours face to face for each interview.
4. The best quality data is gathered face to face.

CREATE THE INTERVIEW GUIDE
1. An interview guide is a set of questions that you plan to ask during the interview.
2. Your interview guide is designed to guide you through the process.
3. An interview guide directs the conversation to make sure that desired content is covered.
4. It creates uniformity when you interview multiple interviewees or have multiple interviewers.

Adapted from Ash Maurya, Running Lean, 2012

PROBLEM DEFINITION INTERVIEW

WHAT
Identify your target audience. Test your assumptions about the audience and their needs. Interview at least ten people. Ask the participants to rank their top three needs. Ask the participant how each problem should be solved. How do the participants solve the problems today?

A SCRIPT FOR THE PROBLEM INTERVIEWS

WELCOME
Explain the interview process and the purpose of the interview.

COLLECT BACKGROUND INFORMATION
Ask introductory questions and collect necessary background information: "Before we go to the problems, I would like to know....how often / with whom / do you...?"

TELL A STORY
Illustrate the top problems you want to explore. "Let me tell you about the problems we are tackling...do any of these resonate with you?"

PROBLEM RANKING
State the top 3 problems and ask the interviewee to rank them. Ask if the interviewee has any other problems related to the issue

EXPLORE CUSTOMER'S WORLDVIEW
Go through each problem and ask the interviewees how they address them today.

WRAP-UP
Ask for permission to follow-up.

DOCUMENT RESULTS.
Document thoughts that you did not have time to write down while interviewing.

Adapted from Ash Maurya, Running Lean, 2012

INTERVIEWING

WHAT
Interviewing is a method of ethnographic research that has been described as a conversation with a purpose.

WHY
1. Contextual interviews uncover tacit knowledge about people's context.
2. The information gathered can be detailed.
3. The information produced by contextual inquiry is relatively reliable

CHALLENGES
1. End users may not have the answers
2. Contextual inquiry may be difficult to challenge even if it is misleading.
3. Keep control
4. Be prepared
5. Be aware of bias
6. Be neutral
7. Select location carefully

WHEN
1. Know Context
2. Know User
3. Frame insights

HOW
1. Contextual inquiry may be structured as 2 hour one on one interviews.
2. The researcher does not usually impose tasks on the user.
3. Go to the user's context. Talk, watch listen and observe.
4. Understand likes and dislikes.
5. Collect stories and insights.
6. See the world from the user's point of view.
7. Take permission to conduct interviews.
8. Do one-on-one interviews.
9. The researcher listens to the user.
10. 2 to 3 researchers conduct an interview.
11. Understand relationship between people, product and context.
12. Document with video, audio and notes.

WRITING AN INTERVIEW GUIDE

HOW
1. Plan in advance what you want to achieve
2. Research the topic
3. Select a person to interview.
4. Meet them in their location if possible.
5. Set a place, date, and time.
6. Be sure he or she understands how long the interview should take and that you plan to record the session.
7. Start with an open-ended question. It is a good way to put the candidate at ease,
8. Tape record the interview if possible.
9. Decide what information you need
10. Write down the information you'd like to collect through the interview. Now frame your interview questions around this information.
11. Prepare follow-up questions to ask.
12. Research the person that you are interviewing
13. Check your equipment and run through your questions.
14. Use neutral wording
15. Do not ask leading questions or questions that show bias.
16. Leave time for a General Question in the End
17. The last question should allow the

interviewee to share any thoughts or opinions that they might want to share, such as "Thank you for all that valuable information, is there anything else you'd like to add before we end?"
18. Bring your questions to the interview
19. Explore the answers but return to your list of questions to follow your guide.
20. Record details such as the subject's name contact and details
21. Take detailed notes
22. Use empathy tools to encourage your participant to share information.
23. Final question: "Is there anything you think I should have asked that I didn't?"
24. Transcribe the interview
25. Write out both sides of the conversation, both question and answer.
26. Never change what the interviewee said or how they said it.
27. Outline the important points.
28. Edit the transcript for clarity, flow, and length.
29. Tell a story
30. Add details from your notes appearance and personality of your subject, ambient sounds, smells, visuals.
31. Check the facts.

Source: adapted from The Art of Interview" by Anne Williams

INTERVIEWING METHODS
CONTEXTUAL INQUIRY

WHAT
Contextual inquiry involves one-on-one observations and interviews of activities in the context. Contextual inquiry has four guiding principles:
1. Context
2. Partnership with users.
3. Interpretation
4. Focus on particular goals.

WHO
Whiteside, Bennet, and Holtzblatt 1988

WHY
1. Contextual interviews uncover tacit knowledge about people's context.
2. The information gathered can be detailed.
3. The information produced by contextual inquiry is relatively reliable

CHALLENGES
1. End users may not have the answers
2. Contextual inquiry may be difficult to challenge even if it is misleading.

HOW
1. Contextual inquiry may be structured as 2 hour one on one interviews.

2. The researcher does not usually impose tasks on the user.
3. Go to the user's context. Talk, watch listen and observe.
4. Understand likes and dislikes.
5. Collect stories and insights.
6. See the world from the user's point of view.
7. Take permission to conduct interviews.
8. Do one-on-one interviews.
9. The researcher listens to the user.
10. 2 to 3 researchers conduct an interview.
11. Understand relationship between people, product and context.
12. Document with video, audio and notes.

CONTEXTUAL LADDERING

WHAT
Contextual laddering is a one-on-one interviewing technique done in context. Answers are further explored by the researcher to uncover root causes or core values.

WHO
Gutman 1982, Olsen and Reynolds 2001.

WHY
1. Laddering can uncover underlying reasons for particular behaviors.
2. Laddering may uncover information not revealed by other methods.
3. Complement other methods
4. Link features and product attributes with user/customer values

CHALLENGES
1. Analysis of data is sometimes difficult.
2. Requires a skilled interviewer who can keep the participants engaged.
3. Laddering may be repetitive
4. Sometimes information may not be represented hierarchically.

HOW
1. Interviews typically take 60 to 90-minutes.
2. The introduction. The researcher gives information about the length of the interview, content, confidentiality and method of recording.
3. The body of the interview. The researcher investigates the user in context and documents the information gathered.
4. Ask participants to describe what kinds of features would be useful in or distinguish different products.
5. Ask why.
6. If this answer doesn't describe the root motivation ask why again.
7. Repeat step 3. until you have reached the root motivation.
8. Wrap up. Verification and clarification

E-MAIL INTERVIEW

WHAT
With this method an interview is conducted via an e-mail exchange.

WHY
1. Extended access to people.
2. Background noises are not

recorded.
3. Interviewee can answer the questions at his or her own convenience
4. It is not necessary to take notes
5. It is possible to use online translators.
6. Interviewees do not have to identify a convenient time to talk.

CHALLENGES
1. Interviewer may have to wait for answers.
2. Interviewer is disconnected from context.
3. Lack of communication of body language.

HOW
1. Choose a topic
2. Identify a subject.
3. Contact subject and obtain approval.
4. Prepare interview questions.
5. Conduct interview
6. Analyze data.

EXTREME USER INTERVIEW

WHAT
Interview experienced or inexperienced users of a product or service in order to discover useful insights that can be applied to the general users.

WHY
Extreme user's solutions to problems can inspire solutions for general users. Their behavior can be more exaggerated than general users so it is sometimes easier to develop useful insights from these groups.

CHALLENGES
1. Keep control
2. Be prepared
3. Be aware of bias
4. Be neutral
5. Select location carefully

HOW
1. Do a timeline of your activity and break it into main activities
2. Identify very experienced or very inexperienced users of a product or service in an activity area.
3. Explore their experiences through interview.
4. Discover insights that can inspire design.
5. Refine design based on insights.

GROUP INTERVIEW

WHAT
This method involves interviewing a group of people.

WHY
People will often give different answers to questions if interviewed on=on=-one and in groups. If resources are available it is useful to interview people in both situations.

CHALLENGES
Group interview process is longer than an individual interview

HOW
1. Welcome everyone and introduce yourself
2. Describe the process.
3. Ask everyone to introduce themselves.
4. Conduct a group activity or warming-up exercise.
5. Break the larger group into

smaller groups of 4 or 5 people and give them a question to answer. Ask each participant to present their response to the larger group.
6. Allow about 25 minutes.
7. Ask each interviewee to write a summary
8. Collect the summaries.
9. Ask if have any further comments.
10. Thank everyone and explain the next steps.
11. Give them your contact details.

GUIDED STORYTELLING

WHAT
Guided storytelling is interview technique, where the designer asks a participant to walk you through a scenario of use for a concept. Directed storytelling guides participants to describe their experiences and thoughts on a particular topic.

WHO
Whiteside, Bennet, and Holtzblatt 1988

WHY
Guided storytelling uncovers tacit knowledge.

CHALLENGES
1. Keep control
2. Be prepared
3. Be aware of bias
4. Be neutral
5. Select location carefully

HOW
1. Contextual inquiry may be structured as 2 hour one on one interviews.
2. The researcher does not usually impose tasks on the user.
3. Go to the user's context. Talk, watch listen and observe.
4. Understand likes and dislikes.
5. Collect stories and insights.
6. See the world from the user's point of view.
7. Take permission to conduct interviews.
8. Do one-on-one interviews.
9. The researcher listens to the user.
10. 2 to 3 researchers conduct an interview.
11. Understand relationship between people, product and context.

MAN IN THE STREET INTERVIEW

WHAT
Man in the street interviews are impromptu interviews recorded on video. They are usually conducted by two people, a researcher and a cameraman.

WHY
1. Contextual interviews uncover tacit knowledge.
2. The information gathered can be detailed.

CHALLENGES
1. Keep control
2. Be prepared
3. Be aware of bias
4. Be neutral
5. Ask appropriate questions
6. Select location carefully

DAY IN THE LIFE

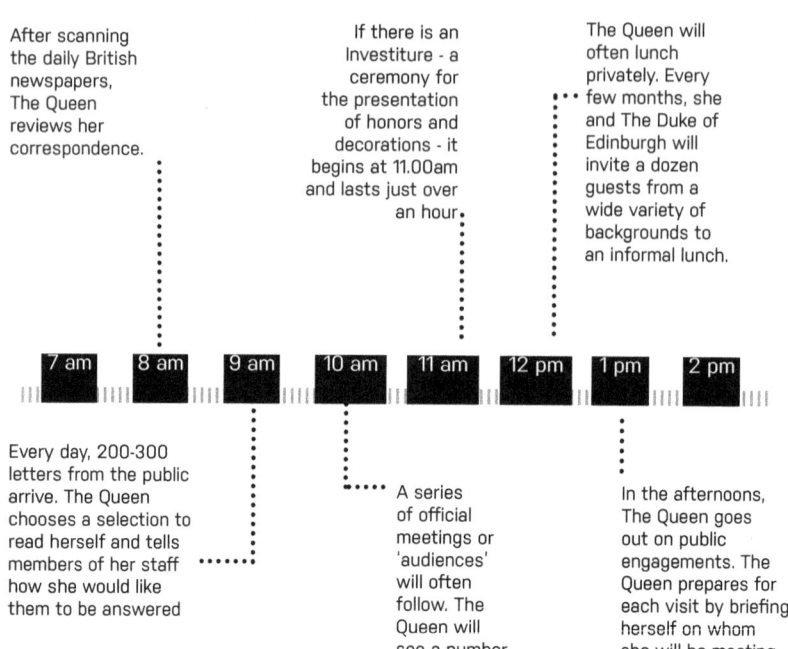

After scanning the daily British newspapers, The Queen reviews her correspondence.

If there is an Investiture - a ceremony for the presentation of honors and decorations - it begins at 11.00am and lasts just over an hour.

The Queen will often lunch privately. Every few months, she and The Duke of Edinburgh will invite a dozen guests from a wide variety of backgrounds to an informal lunch.

7 am | 8 am | 9 am | 10 am | 11 am | 12 pm | 1 pm | 2 pm

Every day, 200-300 letters from the public arrive. The Queen chooses a selection to read herself and tells members of her staff how she would like them to be answered

A series of official meetings or 'audiences' will often follow. The Queen will see a number of important people.

In the afternoons, The Queen goes out on public engagements. The Queen prepares for each visit by briefing herself on whom she will be meeting and what she will be seeing and doing

DISCOVERY PHASE

DOT VOTING

CONCEPT 1
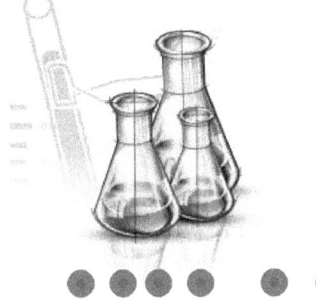
● ● ● ● ● ●

CONCEPT 2

● ●

CONCEPT 3

● ● ● ●

CONCEPT 4

● ● ●

CONCEPT 5

●

CONCEPT 6

● ● ● ● ●

7. Create a friendly atmosphere, interviewee to feel relaxed.
8. Clearly convey the purpose of the interview.
9. This method results in accidental sampling which may not be representative of larger groups.

HOW
1. Decide on goal for research.
2. Formulate about 10 questions related to topic
3. Use release form if required.
4. Conduct a preliminary interview.
5. Select location. It should not be too noisy or have other distracting influences
6. Approach people, be polite. Say, "Excuse me, I work for [your organization] and I was wondering if you could share your opinion about [your topic]."
7. If someone does not wish to respond, select another subject to interview.
8. Limit your time. Each interview should be no be longer than about 10-minutes.
9. Conduct 6 to 10 interviews

NATURALISTIC GROUP INTERVIEW

WHAT
Naturalistic group interview is an interview method where the participants know each other prior to the interview and so have conversations that are more natural than participants who do not know each other.

WHY
1. This method has been applied in research in Asia where beliefs are informed by group interaction.
2. Can help gain useful data in cultures where people are less willing to share their feelings.

CHALLENGES
Familiarity of participants can lead to Group-think.

HOW
1. The interview context should support natural conversation.
2. Select participants who have existing social relationships.
3. Group the participants in natural ways so that the conversation is as close as possible to the type of discussion they would have in their everyday life.
4. Groups should be no larger than four people for best results.

ONE-ON-ONE INTERVIEWS

WHAT
The one-on-one interview is an interview that is between a researcher and one participant in a face-to-face situation.

WHY
1. The best method for personal information
2. Works well with other methods in obtaining information to inform design.
3. Can be used to exchange ideas or to gather information to inform design

CHALLENGES
1. Keep control
2. Be prepared
3. Be aware of bias
4. Be neutral
5. Select location carefully
6. Record everything
7. Combine one on one interviews with group interviews.

HOW
1. May be structured as 2 hour one on one interviews.
2. Select the questions and the subjects carefully.
3. Create interview guide,
4. Conduct a pre-interview to refine the guide.
5. The researcher does not usually impose tasks on the user.
6. Go to the user's context. Talk, watch listen and observe.
7. Understand likes and dislikes.
8. Collect stories and insights.
9. See the world from the user's point of view.
10. Take permission to conduct interviews.
11. Understand relationship between person, product and context.
12. Document with video, audio and notes.

STRUCTURED INTERVIEW

WHAT

In a structured interview, the researcher prepares a list of questions, script or an interview guide that they follow during the interview. Most interviews use a structured method.

INTERVIEW GUIDE
1. 4-5 distinct topics or questions
2. Distinct probes for each topic
3. Specific order
4. Order from general to specific
5. Begin with most important questions
6. Builds in transitions among topics

WHY
1. A structured interview is often used for phone interviews.
2. It is easy to analyze the results.
3. Structured interviews are often used by quantitative researchers.

TESTING THE INTERVIEW GUIDE
1. Are the questions phrased in a way that will elicit the information that you're seeking?
2. Are the questions clear?
3. Are the questions biased?
4. Are any of them closed ended?
5. Do any need expansion?
6. Did you use any double negatives?

CHALLENGES
1. Respondents may be less likely to discuss sensitive experiences.

HOW
1. The researcher should follow the script exactly.
2. The interviewer is required to show consistency in behavior across all interviews

ANALYSIS
1. Familiarization
2. Transcribing
3. Organizing
4. Coding
5. Reducing data
6. Displaying data
   - Helps organize data
   - See areas where analysis is complete

- See patterns & themes
- See how data "fits" theory
7. Drawing & Verifying Conclusions
8. Inductive: categories and themes emerge (grounded theory)
9. Deductive: processes of "fitting" the data into categories and themes (framework analysis)

PHOTO ELICITATION INTERVIEW

WHAT
Photos are used by a researcher as a focus to discuss the experiences, thoughts and feelings of participants.

WHY
1. A method sometimes used to interview children.
2. Photos can make staring a conversation with a participant easier.
3. Photos can uncover meaning which is not uncovered in a face to face interview.

CHALLENGES
1. Photos can create ethical questions for the researcher.
2. A researcher may show bias in selecting subject of photos.

HOW
1. Define the context.
2. Select the participants
3. Either researcher or participant may take the photos.
4. Researcher analyses photos and plans the interview process
5. Researcher shows the photos to the participant and discusses their thoughts in relation to the photographs.
6. The interview is analyzed by the researcher.
7. Create a list of insights.

UNSTRUCTURED INTERVIEW

WHAT
Unstructured interviews are interviews where questions can be modified as needed by the researcher during the interview.

INTERVIEW GUIDE
1-2 broad topics

WHY
1. A useful technique for understanding how a subject may perform under pressure.
2. Unstructured interviews are used in ethnographic case studies
3. Respondents may be more likely to discuss sensitive experiences.

CHALLENGES
1. Interviewer bias is unavoidable.

HOW
Researchers need a list of topics to be covered during the interview.

The interviewer and respondents engage in a formal interview in that they have a scheduled time to sit and speak with each other and both parties recognize this to be an interview.
1. The interviewer has a clear plan of the focus and goal of the interview.
2. There is no interview guide.
3. The interviewer builds rapport with subject.
4. Questions are open-ended.
5. Unstructured interviews are used for developing an understanding of an as-of-yet not fully

understood topic.

TELEPHONE INTERVIEW

WHAT
This style of interview is conducted via telephone.

WHY
Wide geographical access
1. Allows researcher to reach hard to reach people.
2. Allows researcher to access closed locations.
3. Access to dangerous or politically sensitive sites

CHALLENGES
1. Lack of communication of body language.
2. Interviewer is disconnected from context.

HOW
1. Choose a topic
2. Identify a subject.
3. Contact subject and obtain approval.
4. Prepare interview questions.
5. Conduct interview
6. Analyze data.

MIXED METHOD RESEARCH

WHAT
Mixed methods research is a design for collecting, analyzing, and mixing both quantitative and qualitative data in a single study or series of studies to understand a research problem.

Mixed methods research is a systematic integration of quantitative and qualitative methods in a single study for purposes of obtaining a fuller picture and deeper understanding of a phenomenon."

Huey Chen

Mixed methods research is a set of procedures that should be used when integrating qualitative and quantitative procedures reflects the research question(s) better than each can independently. The combining of quantitative and qualitative methods should better inform the researcher and the effectiveness of mixed methods should be evaluated based upon how the approach enables the investigator to answer the research question(s) embedded in the purpose(s) (why the study is being conducted or is needed; the justification) of the study."

Newman, Ridenour, Newman & DeMarco, 2003

Qualitative and quantitative research provide a better understanding of users than either method can provide alone. Mixed methods research is becoming increasingly popular.

> *Combining qualitative and quantitative methods has gained broad appeal in public health research. The key question has become not whether it is acceptable or legitimate to combine methods, but rather how they will be combined to be mutually supportive and how findings achieved through different methods will be integrated."*

NIH, Office of Behavioral and Social Science Research

QUALITATIVE:
1. Working with unfamiliar subjects.
2. When data is complex ambiguous or unclear
3. When you wish to understand meaning.
4. When you require flexibility.
5. For studying issues in detail

QUANTITATIVE
1. When the data is clearly defined
2. When metrics are known
3. When detailed numerical data is required
4. When repeatability is important
5. When generalizable across populations is needed

WHY USE MIXED METHODS?
Greene, Caracelli, and Graham (1989) identified the five purposes or rationales of mixed methodological studies:
1. Triangulation (i.e., seeking convergence and corroboration of results from different methods studying the same phenomenon),
2. Complementarity (i.e., seeking elaboration, enhancement, illustration, clarification of the results from one method with results from the other method),
3. Development (i.e., using the results from one method to other method),
4. Initiation (i.e., discovering paradoxes and contradictions that lead to a reframing of the research question), and
5. Expansion (i.e., seeking to expand the breadth and range of inquiry by using different methods for different inquiry components).

WHEN TO USE IT
1. When you want to combine the advantages of quantitative (trends, large numbers, generalization) with qualitative (detail, small numbers, in-depth)
2. When you want to validate your findings
3. When you want to expand your quantitative findings
4. Both approaches have strengths and weaknesses

Some research methods such as interviews and observations can be either quantitative or qualitative. Quantitative data can be generalized to the larger population. In qualitative research subjects are selected because they have experienced the central phenomenon.

WHY USE MIXED METHODS?
1. Together quantitative and qualitative data provide both precise measurement and generalizability of quantitative research and the in-depth, complex picture of qualitative research
2. To validate quantitative results with qualitative data
3. Our quantitative data provide a general explanation and we need

to follow-up with participants and have them explain the quantitative results
4. When outcomes to be measured are not enough; and need to be complemented by understanding
5. Quantitative data may fail to provide specific reasons, explanations or examples
6. Qualitative research provides data about meaning and context
7. Findings are often not generalizable because of the small numbers & narrow range of participants
8. Qualitative research can provide specific examples of quantitative data.
9. Wit quantitative research it may be difficult to see the overall pattern
10. Selection of research methods should be made after the research questions are asked
11. Some methods work well in some contexts but not in other contexts
12. Mixed methods are used when one method only was is insufficient
13. If the results lead to divergent results, then more than one explanation is possible

SATURATION
Saturation occurs:
1. When no new information (redundancy) is obtained *Source Lincoln & Guba, 1985; Patton, 1990*
2. Through the constant comparison of data Recurrent patterns and themes are seen

Source Glaser & Strauss, 1967, Cutcliffe & McKenna, 2002

MOBILE DIARY STUDY

WHAT
A mobile diary studies is a method that uses portable devices to capture a person's experiences in context when and where they happen such as their workplace or home. Participants can create diary entries from their location on mobile phones or tablets.

WHY
1. Most people carry a mobile phone.
2. It is a convenient method of recording diary entries.
3. It is easier to collect the data than collecting written diaries.
4. Collection of data happens in real time.
5. Mobile devices have camera, voice and written capability.

CHALLENGES
1. Can miss non-verbal feedback.
2. Technology may be unreliable.

HOW
1. Define intent
2. Define audience
3. Define context
4. Select the online diary study tool based.
5. Set up the diary study tool, create user accounts, and design study activities
6. Prepare introductory email or letter to participants, with study details and dates
7. Prepare the diary kit
    - User account online login details
    - Types of feedback
    - Contact details
    - Information about what to do regarding additional

questions, user account issues,
8. Conduct online Meet & Brief sessions with participants
9. Create activity and assignment prompts can be written or video.
10. Monitor diary entries and maintain engagement with participants to keep them on task
11. Update and set next tasks
12. Respond to participant inquiries, diary entries, or ensure technical support issues are being resolved
13. Pose additional questions or suggest alternative scenarios to gain deeper insights
14. Make notes and compile data to refer to for follow-up interviews and final data insights report
15. Conduct timely, final in-depth interviews to further probe and validate data revealed during the study
16. Thank participants and ensure compensation is given as applicable

BENEFITS
1. Participants record their experiences in their natural environment rather than an unrelated, unnatural environment such as a lab.
2. Participants more likely to capture influential external factors such as time, location, social or environmental triggers, etc.
3. Researchers can collect participant observations in longer durations + Diary studies offer participants more time for in-depth consideration and opportunities for creativity than traditional-type research sessions, allowing participants a few days per activity/question

DRAWBACKS
1. Researchers do not observe participants in their natural environment or collect their own real-time data
2. Participants may have a belief bias, adjust behaviors, or have difficulty recalling events
3. Researchers must trust participants on what they record or observe about their experiences and emotional behaviors
4. Finding the right respondents who can be creative is a MUST, which means recruiting might take longer to avoid selecting candidates that might plateau or withdraw before the study is complete

SAMPLE INTERVIEW CONSENT FORM

Research should, be based on participants' freely volunteered informed consent. The researcher has a responsibility to explain what the research is about and who will see the data. Participants should be aware that they can refuse to participate; confidentiality, and how the research will be used.

The information contained within this book is strictly for educational purposes. If you wish to apply ideas contained in this book you are taking full responsibility for your actions. There are no representations or warranties, express or implied, about the completeness, accuracy, reliability, suitability or availability with respect to the information, products, services, or related graphics contained in this book for any purpose. Any use of this information is at your own risk.

Purpose of the research
The purpose of this project is [purpose]. *Provide a brief, usually one-paragraph, explanation of what the research is about and state why the subject is being asked to participate [e.g., inclusion/exclusion criteria]*

What we will ask you to do
If you agree to be in this study, you are asked to participate in a recorded interview. The interview will include questions about [topic] , The interview will take about [duration] minutes to complete. With your permission, we would also like to tape-record the interview.

Risks and benefits
There is the risk that you may find some of the questions about [topic] to be sensitive. *[Describe any possible benefit to the participants or others that may reasonably be expected from the research; then describe any reasonably foreseeable risks or discomforts to the participants, or state "there are no foreseeable risks," if none are identified.]*

Compensation:
There will be [amount of compensation] [type of compensation] compensation. *[Specify whether participants will be compensated and if so, the amount. If amount will be prorated for any reason, state this.]*

Taking part is voluntary
Taking part in this interview is completely voluntary. You may skip any questions that you do not want to answer. If you decide not to take part or to skip some of the questions, it will not affect your current or future relationship with Cornell University. If you decide to take part, you are free to withdraw at any time.

Your answers will be confidential
The records of this project will be kept private. In any sort of report we make public we will not include any information that will make it possible to identify you. Research records will be kept in a locked file; only [who] will have access to the records. [Regarding the storage of the tape, who will keep it, where will it be stored, after the transcription is done?] If we tape-record the interview, we will destroy the tape after it has been transcribed, which we anticipate will be within [duration] months of its taping.
If you have questions: [contact]

If you have questions
The researchers conducting this study are [researchers]. Please ask any questions you have now. If you have questions later, you may contact [name] at [email] or at [phone].

Statement of Consent
I have read the above information, and have received answers to any questions I asked. I consent to take part in the project. In addition to agreeing to participate, I also consent to having the interview tape-recorded. I understand the information presented above and that: My participation is voluntary, and I may withdraw my consent and discontinue participation in the project at any time. My refusal to participate will not result in any penalty.

You will be given a copy of this form to keep for your records.

Interviewee Signature ....Date ....
In addition to agreeing to participate, I also consent to having the interview tape-recorded.

Researcher's Signature ....Date ....
This consent form will be kept by the researcher for at least [duration] years beyond the end of the project and was approved by the [Organization] on [date].

This consent form will be kept by the researcher for at least [duration] years beyond the end of the project and was approved by the [Organization] on [date].

MYSTERY SHOPPER

WHAT

Mystery Shopping is a method used to anonymously evaluate products and services, operations, employee integrity, merchandising, and product quality. Mystery shoppers perform tasks such as purchasing a product, asking questions, registering complaints and then provide feedback about their experiences. Mystery shopping evaluation generates around $1.5 billion per annum and is growing.

MYSTERY SHOPPING IS ALSO KNOWN AS:
1. Secret Shopping
2. Experience Evaluation
3. Anonymous Audits
4. Mystery Customers
5. Digital Customers
6. Virtual Customers

WHO

Originally used in the 1940s as a way of evaluating employee integrity.n the 1940's, Wilmark coined the term "mystery shopping". In the 1970's and 80's, Shop 'n Chek popularized mystery shopping. Since 2010, mystery shopping has become a common form of evaluation in the medical tourism industry and in the UK in customer services provided by local authorities and other non-profit organizations such as housing associations and churches. some fast-food restaurants are mystery-shopped three times a day and shoppers are rotated.

Source: Newhouse 2004: 2

WHO USES MYSTERY SHOPPING?
User include:
1. Banks
2. Gas stations
3. Retailers
4. Car dealers
5. Apartments
6. Manufacturers
7. Call Centers
8. E-Commerce services
9. Government agencies
10. Hospitals
11. Associations
12. Franchise operations
13. Promotions agencies Hotels
14. Restaurants
15. Movie Theaters
16. Recreation parks
17. Transportation systems
18. Fitness/health centers
19. Property management firms
20. Freight/courier services

WHO PROVIDES MYSTERY SHOPPING SERVICES?
21. Consultants
22. Marketing Firms
23. Private Investigators
24. Merchandising Companies
25. Advertising agencies

CHALLENGES
1. Time-consuming
2. Employees may resist
3. Ethical management

BENEFITS OF MYSTERY SHOPPING
1. Metrics for service performance.
2. Improves customer retention.
3. Ensures service quality..
4. Competitive analyses.
5. Compliments marketing research data.
6. Identifies training needs and sales opportunities.
7. Educational tool.
8. Monitors employee integrity.

USE OF THE INTERNET
1. Many websites use mystery shopping.
2. May be easier to implement online.

HOW
1. Define objectives.
2. Program & questionnaire design.
3. Create evaluation form for mystery shopper.
4. Recruit shoppers.
5. Train shoppers.
6. Conduct evaluation.
7. Analyze data.
8. Report conclusions and recommendations.
9. Review findings.
10. Implement actions.

OBJECTIVES & GOALS
Identify and define actionable goals.

QUESTIONNAIRE DESIGN
11. Design questionnaires to provide objective, observational feedback
12. Cover: greeting, customer service, facility cleanliness and orderliness, speed of service, product quality and employee product knowledge
13. Ask only "yes" and "no" questions. Ask for clarification of no questions.
14. Include a "general comments" section
15. Use a scoring system. Give a weighting to the most important questions.

RECRUITING SHOPPERS
1. Mystery shoppers should match "real customer" profiles.
2. Mystery shoppers are often employed as part-time contractors.
3. Recruit through classified advertising, Internet or referrals.
4. There may be special requirements such as wearing glasses.
5. Shoppers may be asked to complete test shops during recruiting.

DATA COLLECTION
1. Provide shoppers with specific shopping tasks and clear written guidelines
2. Be consistent
3. Mystery shopper observations are limited to a choice of fixed alternatives

DATA PREPARATION
1. Check and validate each report.
2. Run quality control checks
3. Track data using relational database.

REPORTING
1. Process reports within 30 days.
2. The reports should be actionable.

REVIEW FINDINGS
1. Share the reports with training personnel.
2. An ongoing program is more effective than irregular audits.

HOW TO CHOOSE A MYSTERY SHOPPING PROVIDER
3. Experience
4. Reputation
5. Resources
6. Location

HOW TO MAKE THE MOST OF MYSTERY SHOPPING PROGRAMS
1. Inform employees of the program.
2. Promote the program.
3. Action the findings.
4. Take a positive approach.
5. Apply to employee training.
6. Share the findings
7. Evaluate only actionable issues.
8. Use yes/no questions
9. Limit use of open questions.

10. Benchmark and track trends.

Source: Adapted from Mark Michelson

OBSERVATION

WHAT
This method involves observing people in their natural activities and usual context such as work environment. With direct observation the researcher is present and indirect observation the activities may be recorded by means such as video or digital voice recording.

WHY
1. Allows the observer to view what users actually do in context.
2. Indirect observation uncovers activity that may have previously gone unnoticed

CHALLENGES
1. Observation does not explain the cause of behavior.
2. Obtrusive observation may cause participants to alter their behavior.
3. Analysis can be time-consuming.
4. Observer bias can cause the researcher to look only where they think they will see useful information.

HOW
1. Define objectives
2. Define participants and obtain their cooperation.
3. Define The context of the observation: time and place.
4. In some countries the law requires that you obtain written consent to video people.
5. Define the method of observation and the method of recording information. Common methods are taking written notes, video or audio recording.
6. Run a test session.
7. Hypothesize an explanation for the phenomenon
8. Predict a logical consequence of the hypothesis
9. Test your hypothesis by observation
10. Analyze the data gathered and create a list of insights derived from the observations.

RESOURCES
Notepad computer
Pens
Camera
Video camera
Digital voice recorder

COVERT OBSERVATION

WHAT
Covert observation is to observe people without them knowing. The identity of the researcher and the purpose of the research are hidden from the people being observed.

WHY
1. This method may be used to reduce the effect of the observer's presence on the behavior of the subjects.
2. To capture behavior as it happens.
3. Researcher is more likely to observe natural behavior

CHALLENGES
1. The method raises serious ethical questions.
2. Observation does not explain the cause of behavior.
3. Can be difficult to gain access and maintain cover
4. Analysis can be time-consuming.
5. Observer bias can cause the researcher to look only where they think they will see useful information.

HOW
1. Define objectives.
2. Define participants and obtain their cooperation.
3. Define The context of the observation: time and place.
4. In some countries the law requires that you obtain written consent to video people.
5. Define the method of observation and the method of recording information. Common methods are taking written notes, video or audio recording.
6. Run a test session.
7. Hypothesize an explanation for the phenomenon.
8. Predict a logical consequence of the hypothesis.
9. Test your hypothesis by observation
10. Analyze the data gathered and create a list of insights derived from the observations.

RESOURCES
Camera
Video Camera
Digital voice recorder

DIRECT OBSERVATION

WHAT
Direct Observation is a method in which a researcher observes and records behavior events, activities or tasks while something is happening recording observations as they are made.

WHO
Radcliff-Brown 1910
Bronisław Malinowski 1922
Margaret Mead 1928

WHY
To capture behavior as it happens.

CHALLENGES
1. Observation does not explain the cause of behavior.
2. Analysis can be time-consuming.
3. Observer bias can cause the researcher to look only where they think they will see useful information.
4. Obtain a proper sample for generalization.
5. Observe average workers during average conditions.
6. The participant may change their behavior because they are being watched.

HOW
1. Define objectives.
2. Make direct observation plan
3. Define participants and obtain their cooperation.
4. Define The context of the observation: time and place.

5. In some countries, the law requires that you obtain written consent to video people.
6. Define the method of observation and the method of recording information. Common methods are taking written notes, video or audio recording.
7. Run a test session.
8. Hypothesize an explanation for the phenomenon.
9. Predict a logical consequence of the hypothesis.
10. Test your hypothesis by observation
11. Analyze the data gathered and create a list of insights derived from the observations.

RESOURCES
Notepad computer
Pens
Camera
Video Camera
Digital voice recorder

INDIRECT OBSERVATION

WHAT
Indirect Observation is an observational technique whereby some record of past behavior is used than observing behavior in real time. Humans cannot directly sense some things, we must rely on indirect observations with tools such as thermometers, microscopes, telescopes or X-rays.

WHY
1. To capture behavior or an event as it happens in it's natural setting.

2. Indirect observation uncovers activity that may have previously gone unnoticed
3. May be inexpensive
4. Can collect a wide range of data

CHALLENGES
1. Observation does not explain the cause of behavior.
2. Analysis can be time-consuming.
3. Observer bias can cause the researcher to look only where they think they will see useful information.
4. Observe average workers during average conditions.
5. The participant may change their behavior because they are being watched.

HOW
1. Define objectives.
2. Make direct observation plan
3. Define participants and obtain their cooperation.
4. Define The context of the observation: time and place.
5. In some countries the law requires that you obtain written consent to video people.
6. Define the method of observation and the method of recording information.
7. Run a test session.
8. Hypothesize an explanation for the phenomenon.
9. Predict a logical consequence of the hypothesis.
10. Test your hypothesis by observation
11. Analyze the data gathered and create a list of insights derived from the observations.

NON-PARTICIPANT

OBSERVATION

WHAT
The observer does not become part of the situation being observed or intervene in the behavior of the subjects. Used when a researcher wants the participants to behave normally. Usually this type of observation occurs in places where people normally work or live.

WHY
12. To capture behavior as it happens.

CHALLENGES
1. Observation does not explain the cause of behavior.
2. Analysis can be time-consuming.
3. Observer bias can cause the researcher to look only where they think they will see useful information.
4. Obtain a proper sample for generalization.
5. Observe average workers during average conditions.
6. The participant may change their behavior because they are being watched.

HOW
1. Determine research goals.
2. Select a research context
3. The site should allow clear observation and be accessible.
4. Select participants
5. Seek permission.
6. Gain access
7. Gather research data.
8. Analyze data
9. Find common themes
10. Create insights

PARTICIPANT OBSERVATION

WHAT
Participant observation is an observation method where the researcher participates. The researcher becomes part of the situation being studied. The researcher may live or work in the context of the participant and may become an accepted member of the participant's community. This method was used extensively by the pioneers of field research.

WHO
Radcliff-Brown 1910
Bronisław Malinowski 1922
Margaret Mead 1928

WHY
1. The goal of this method is to become close and familiar with the behavior of the participants.
2. To capture behavior as it happens.

CHALLENGES?
1. May be time-consuming.
2. May be costly.
3. The researcher may influence the behavior of the participants.
4. The participants may not show the same behavior if the observer was not present.
5. May be language barriers.
6. May be cultural barriers.
7. May be risks for the researcher.
8. May be sensitive to privacy, and confidentiality.

HOW
1. Determine research goals.
2. Select a research context
3. The site should allow clear observation and be accessible.

4. Select participants
5. Seek permission.
6. Gain access
7. Gather research data.
8. Analyze data
9. Find common themes
10. Create insights

OVERT OBSERVATION

WHAT
A method of observation where the subjects are aware that they are being observed.

WHO
Radcliff-Brown 1910
Bronisław Malinowski 1922
Margaret Mead 1928

WHY
To capture behavior as it happens.

CHALLENGES
1. Observation does not explain the cause of behavior.
2. Analysis can be time-consuming.
3. Observer bias can cause the researcher to look only where they think they will see useful information.

HOW
1. Define objectives.
2. Define participants and obtain their cooperation.
3. Define The context of the observation: time and place.
4. In some countries the law requires that you obtain written consent to video people.
5. Define the method of observation and the method of recording information. Common methods are taking written notes, video or audio recording.
6. Run a test session.
7. Hypothesize an explanation for the phenomenon.
8. Predict a logical consequence of the hypothesis.
9. Test your hypothesis by observation
10. Analyze the data gathered and create a list of insights derived from the observations.

STRUCTURED OBSERVATION

WHAT
Particular types of behavior are observed and counted like a survey. The observer may create an event so that the behavior can be more easily studied. This approach is systematically planned and executed.

WHY
1. Allows stronger generalizations than unstructured observation.
2. May allow an observer to study behavior that may be difficult to study in unstructured observation.
3. To capture behavior as it happens.
4. A procedure is used which can be replicated.

CHALLENGES
1. Observation does not explain the cause of behavior.
2. Analysis can be time-consuming.
3. Observer bias can cause the researcher to look only where they think they will see useful information.

HOW
1. Define objectives.
2. Define participants and obtain their cooperation.
3. Define The context of the observation: time and place.
4. In some countries the law requires that you obtain written consent to video people.
5. Define the method of observation and the method of recording information. Common methods are taking written notes, video or audio recording.
6. Run a test session.
7. Hypothesize an explanation for the phenomenon.
8. Predict a logical consequence of the hypothesis.
9. Test your hypothesis by observation
10. Analyze the data gathered and create a list of insights derived from the observations.

UNSTRUCTURED OBSERVATION

WHAT
This method is used when a researcher wants to see what is naturally occurring without predetermined ideas. We use have an open-ended approach to observation and record all that we observe.

WHY
1. To capture behavior as it happens.
2. Observation is the most direct measure of behavior

CHALLENGES
1. Replication may be difficult.
2. Observation does not explain the cause of behavior.
3. Analysis can be time-consuming.
4. Observer bias can cause the researcher to look only where they think they will see useful information.
5. Data cannot be quantified
6. In this form of observation there is a higher probability of observer's bias.

HOW
1. Select a context to explore
2. Take a camera, note pad and pen
3. Record things and questions that you find interesting
4. Record ideas as you form them
5. Do not reach conclusions.
6. Ask people questions and try to understand the meaning in their replies.

PERSONAL INVENTORY

WHAT
This method involves studying the contents of a research subject's purse, or wallet. Study the things that they carry every day.

WHO
Rachel Strickland and Doreen Nelson 1998

WHY
1. To provide insights into the user's lifestyle, activities, perceptions, and values.
2. To understand the needs priorities and interests.

HOW
1. Formulate aims of research

2. Recruit participants carefully.
3. Document the contents with photographs and notes
4. ask your research subject to talk about the objects and their meaning.
5. Analyze the data.

> *The participant is asked to bring their 'most often carried bag' and lay the objects they carry on a flat surface, talking through the purpose and last-use of each item. Things to look out for where the bag is kept in the home and what is clustered around it, what is packed/repacked on arrival/departure, and the use of different bags for different activities."*
>
> Jan Chipchase

RESOURCES
Camera
Notepad computer

PROBLEM DEFINITION INTERVIEW

WHAT
The problem interview is all about testing your assumptions about a problem and to whom it is a problem.

HOW
State the top 1-3 problems and ask the interviewee to rank them.
Go through each problem and ask the interviewees how they address them today. General rule of thumb: you are done with the problem interviews when.
6. You have a must-have problem.
7. You can identify the demographics.
8. Of an early adopter
9. You can describe how customers.
10. Solve this problem today
11. You should interview at least ten people.

A SCRIPT FOR THE PROBLEM INTERVIEWS

WELCOME: SET THE STAGE.
Shortly, explain how the interview works. "Thank you for taking the time…We are currently…."

COLLECT BACKGROUND INFORMATION
Ask introductory questions and collect necessary background information: "Before we go to the problems, I would like to know….how often / with whom / do you…?"

TELL A STORY TO SET THE CONTEXT
Illustrate the top problems you want to explore with your interviewee. "Let me tell you about the problems we are tackling…do any of these resonate with you?"

PROBLEM RANKING
State the top 1-3 problems and ask the interviewee to rank them. Ask if the interviewee has any other problems related to the discussed issue that she would like to add.

EXPLORE CUSTOMER'S WORLD-VIEW

Go through each problem and ask the interviewees how they address them today. Let them go to as much detail as they wish. Consider (and ask if necessary) how they rate the problems:
"must-have", "nice to have", or "don't need".

WRAP-UP

If you have a solution already in mind, give a conceptual description of what you have in mind in order to maintain
interest. Then ask for permission to follow-up.

DOCUMENT RESULTS.

Take a few minutes to document your thoughts, that you did not have time to write down while interviewing.

Adapted from Ash Maurya, Running Lean, 2012

RECRUITMENT BRIEF

At the beginning of each phase, you must work as a team to:

1. Write your research questions
2. Decide what user research activities will help you answer your questions
3. Identify the target audience.
4. Decide recruitment method
5. Review your research.
6. Select your space and gather your materials.

A recruitment brief is the instructions that you will send to a recruiting company.
They will create a screener.

Always provide the agency with a written brief.

In your brief, you should cover:
1. Research dates.
2. Research location
3. The number of participants
4. A description of the people you would like to recruit.
5. Incentives

REVIEWING THE SCREENER

The agency will provide you with a screener. Check the screener to ensure that it aligns with your needs.

SERVICE SAFARI

WHAT

A service safari is a research method for understanding services. By using a service you will be able to understand how that service works and what the experience is like. A service safari could be used to find out information about a specific service.

When carrying out a service safari you should think about:
6. Different stages which make up the service
7. People involved in delivering the service and what they do
8. What objects you use or interact with
9. What spaces the service takes place in
10. What information is available to people
11. How people involved in delivering the
12. Service contribute to the experience.

Taking photos or video will help you to find out more about the service you are using

HOW
1. What is the service?
2. What information is there?
3. What makes this service work well?
4. What are users doing?
5. What products are used?
6. What makes this service not work well?
7. Who is involved?
8. What is the space like?

SHADOWING

WHAT
Shadowing is observing people in context. The researcher accompanies the user and observes user experiences and activities. It allows the researcher and designer to develop design insights through observation and shared experiences with users.

WHO
Alex Bavelas 1944
Lucy Vernile, Robert A. Monteiro 1991

WHY
1. This method can help determine the difference between what subjects say they do and what they really do.
2. It helps in understanding the point of view of people. Successful design results from knowing the users.
3. Define intent
4. Can be used to evaluate concepts.

CHALLENGES
1. Selecting the wrong people to shadow.
2. Hawthorne Effect, The observer can influence the daily activities under being studied.

HOW
1. Prepare
2. Select carefully who to shadow.
3. Observe people in context by members of your design team.
4. Capture behaviors that relate to product function.
5. Identify issues and user needs.
6. Create design solutions based on observed and experienced user needs.
7. Typical periods can be one day to one week.

RESOURCES
Video camera
Digital still camera
Notepad computer
Laptop Computer

MAPPING METHODS

CURRENT STATE MAPS
With a current-state journey map, you can:
1. Identify pain points and their causes.
2. Identify gaps in what you are offering customers.
3. Improve the efficiency and effectiveness of a current service or customer experience.
4. Craft a better customer experience for a product service or brand.
5. Plan systematically what your organization is delivering to customers.
6. Implement a more efficient system of touchpoints.
7. Understand how customers behave across multiple channels.
8. Identify where your current customer experience or service is most likely to fail.

9. Unite your team with the common goal of a better customer experience.
10. Identify opportunities for feedback or measurement.
11. Develop metrics for progress towards goals.
12. Align your organization with a better customer experience.

FUTURE STATE MAPS
1. With a future-state journey map, you can:
2. Plan a future service or customer experience.
3. Define a new service with better customer experience than your existing service.
4. Implement a new service or customer experience.
5. Develop a product or service road-map.
6. Envision the ideal customer experience or service.
7. Identify the infrastructure needed to create a new service or customer experience.
8. Plan for hiring new staff
9. Drive positive change in your organization.
10. Develop empathy for customers.

WHAT'S THE DIFFERENCE, BETWEEN A BLUEPRINT AND A JOURNEY MAP?

A customer journey map captures how your customer is feeling emotionally across touchpoints over time.

A service blueprint captures the service or experience delivery process across touch points and the elements that make up the service including the things customers see and do not see.

The two types of maps complement each other. The order in which you create them depends on your goals.

SERVICE BLUEPRINT
1. Define employees roles about the customer experience.
2. Identify areas of service improvement.
3. Identify points where moments of truth will occur.
4. Capturing Dynamic Processes
5. Service blueprinting allows the capturing of dynamic processes in a visual manner.
6. A blueprint is one of few methods that allow you to visually convey events that change over time.
7. Relatively few methods allow for this type of dynamic, and at the same time visual, representation.
8. To identify where your customer experience is most likely to fail.
9. Opportunities for improvements
10. To plan and implement a new customer experience.
11. To implement metrics to measure your customer experience.
12. To audit and improve your service evidence or touchpoints.

JOURNEY MAP
1. To identify customer pain points and gaps in your touchpoints
2. To design a new service or experience with a focus on optimizing your customer's experience.
3. To audit the customer experience.
4. To develop new touch points to improve the customer experience.

USER STORIES

WHAT
User stories describe a user and the reason why they need to use the service you're building. You must use user stories when building your service - they're essential to building and running a service that meets user needs.

WHAT TO INCLUDE
They should include:
1. The person using the service (the actor)
2. What the user needs the service for (the narrative)
3. Why the user needs it (the goal)

FORMAT
They have the following format:

As a... [who is the user?]

I needxxxx
So thatxxxx

FOCUS ON THE GOAL
The most important part of a user story is the goal. This helps you:

Make sure you're solving the need
Decide when the story is done and a user need is met
If you're struggling to write the goal then you should reconsider why you think you need that feature.

WHAT-HOW-WHY

WHAT
The What-How-Why method is a tool to help develop a deeper understanding of stakeholders.

You start with concrete observing what the behavior is then How the person is behaving then finally go to and then finally develop a model for Why. What are the underlying factors driving the behavior?

HOW
You should divide activities into What, How and Why.

4. Record concrete observations of what is happening. What is the person doing? What is happening in the background? What is the person holding? Try to be as objective as possible.

5. How is the person doing what they are doing? Record how the person is doing their activity. Try to describe the emotional impact of performing the task.

6. Develop a theory for why the person is doing what they are doing? What are the underlying emotional drivers behind what you have observed? Make educated guesses regarding motivation and emotions.

7. Test your assumptions with stakeholders.

Source: adapted from Rikke Dam and Teo Siang, Interactive Design Foundation

DISCOVERY PHASE

WWWWWH

WHAT

Who, What, Where, When, Why, and How? is a method for getting a thorough understanding of the problem, It is used to obtain basic information in police investigations. A well-known golden rule of journalism is that if you want to know the full story about something you have to answer all the five W's. Journalists argue your story isn't complete until you answer all six questions.
1. Who is involved?
2. What occurred?
3. When did it happen?
4. Where did it happen?
5. Why did it occur?

WHO
Hermagoras of Temnos, Greece 1st century BC.

WHY
This method helps create a story that communicates clearly the nature of an activity or event to stakeholders.

HOW
1. Ask the questions starting with the 5 w's and 1 h question words.
2. Identify the people involved
3. Identify the activities and make a list of them.
4. Identify all the places and make a list of them.
5. Identify all the time factors and make a list of them.
6. Identify causes for events of actions and make a list of them.
7. Identify the way events took place and make a list of them.
8. Study the relationships between the information.

> *I keep six honest serving men. They taught me all I knew. Their names are what and why and when and how and where and who."*
>
> Rudyard Kipling

SOME WWWWWH QUESTIONS

WHO
1. Who is affected?
2. Who believes that the problem affects them?
3. Needs the problem solved?
4. Does not want the problem to be solved?
5. Could stand in the way of a solution?

WHEN
1. Does it happen
2. Doesn't it happen?
3. Did it start?
4. Will it end?
5. Is the solution needed?
6. Might it happen in the future?
7. Will it be a bigger problem?
8. Will it improve?

WHERE
1. Does it happen?
2. Doesn't it happen
3. Else does it happen?
4. Is the best place to solve the problem

WHY
1. Is this situation a problem?
2. Do you want to solve it?
3. Do you not want to solve it?
4. Does it not go away?
5. Would someone else want to solve it?
6. Can it be solved?
7. Is it difficult to solve?

WHAT
1. May be different in the future
2. Are its weaknesses?
3. Do you like?
4. Makes you unhappy about it?
5. Is flexible?
6. Is not flexible?
7. Do you know?
8. Do you not understand?
9. How have you solved similar problems?
10. Are the underlying ideas?
11. Are the values involved?
12. Are the elements of the problem and how are they related?
13. What can you assume to be correct
14. Is most important
15. Is least important
16. Are your goals?
17. Do you need to discover?

DISCOVERY PHASE

AFFINITY DIAGRAMS

THE ORIGIN OF AFFINITY DIAGRAMS

Jiro Kawakita, Born on November 11 , 1920 - died July 8 , 2009, is a Japanese ethnographer , the first person in ethnogeography in Japan and a researcher in Nepal, inventor of the Affinity diagram. He studied geography at Kyoto University , and also obtained a degree in literature. His achievements have immensely contributed to design thinking, research, ethnography, innovation and solving complex human problems. His work allows designers to make sense from the chaos of real-world complex or wicked problems. His method is perhaps the most basic tool of design thinking. In the 1950s, he did field work in the Sikha Valley in South-Eastern Annapurna, Nepal. Jiro Kawakita was a pioneer in participation of remote Nepalese villagers in researching their problems, to improve water supplies and transport across mountain gorges. He developed empathy by working with the villagers. He practiced what he called a "Key Problem Approach". His approach is what design thinking calls co-design today. This work was the starting point of the KJ method and diagram , which he developed in Japan. Affinity diagrams were introduced to the western world by Shoji Shiba as as one of seven total quality management tools from 1985.

USE AN AFFINITY DIAGRAM WHEN:
1. You are confronted with many facts or ideas in apparent chaos.
2. Issues seem too large and complex to grasp.

Anyone who uses brainstorming can use an affinity diagram. Affinity diagrams, allow large numbers of ideas to be sorted into groups for review and analysis. These, simple diagrams are useful with large group where ideas which are generated at a fast pace need to be organized. The best results are achieved when the activity is completed by a cross-functional team, including key stakeholders. The process requires becoming deeply immersed in the data

BOOKS
- His two books entitled "Journals of Expedition to the Nepali Kingdom" and "Land of Platform Burial" became best sellers in Japan.
-
-

AFFINITY DIAGRAMS

WHAT

An affinity diagram is a method used to organize many ideas into groups with common themes or relationships. Affinity diagrams are tools for analyzing large amounts of data and discovering relationships which allow a design direction to be established based on the associations. This method may uncover significant hidden relationships.

Traditional design methods struggle when dealing with complex or chaotic problems or with large amounts of data. The affinity diagram organizes a large quantity of information by natural relationships. This method taps a team's analytical thinking as well as creativity and intuition. It was invented in the 1960s by Japanese anthropologist Jiro Kawakita and is sometimes referred to as the KJ Method.

You can use an affinity diagram to:
1. Understand what is most important from ambiguous data.
2. Tame complexity.
3. Identify connections in data
4. Create hierarchies.
5. Identifying themes.

Identify what factors to focus on that will support the most successful design possible from a customer's perspective.

Most groups that use this technique are amazed at how powerful and valuable a tool it is. Try it once with an open mind and you'll be another convert."

Nancy R. Tague

For around 50 years affinity diagrams have been an essential pillar of what is known as the Seven Management and Planning Tools, used in Japan. The seven management and planning tools are used in leading global organizations for making and implementing better team decisions.

Jiro Kawakita developed the method, and so it was sometimes referred to as the K-J method.

The affinity diagram is a method that an individual or team can use for problem-solving. Affinity diagrams encourage creative input by everyone on the team.

The tool is used in project

management to sort brainstorming ideas into groups, based on their natural relationships and for synthesis and analysis. It is also used in design research to synthesize insights from field research. Affinity diagrams are built through consensus of a design team on how the information should be grouped in logical ways.

MATERIALS
Three pads of sticky notes. I use yellow notes for the initial data, blue for the headers and pink for the superheaders. If I am working with half a dozen or more people I will start by giving each participant a block of yellow sticky notes and a black pointed sharpie. I prefer a mobile white board as a working surface. If you use a white board have some white board markers.

MATERIALS
I allow about 15 to 20 minutes for the first recording of data, 15 to 20 minutes for the clustering and headers and another 15 minutes for each level of superheaders. The process to create a diagram might take between 40 and 80 minutes depending on the complexity of the data.

WHY USE AFFINITY DIAGRAMS?
Traditional design methods do not work when dealing with complex or chaotic problems with large amounts of data. This tool helps to establish relationships or similarities between many pieces of information. From these relationships, insights can be determined which are the starting point of design solutions. It is possible using this method to reach consensus faster than many other methods.

You can use an affinity diagram to:
1. Understand what is most important from a large amount of complex or ambiguous data.
2. Tame complexity.
3. Understand connections between ideas.
4. Identify relationships in data.
5. Create hierarchies.
6. Exercise team decision-making.
7. Make sense from brainstorming ideas.
8. Support design and data workshops.
9. Identifying themes from data
10. Identify patterns from data.
11. It helps to reduce "team paralysis," from too many options and lack of consensus.

HISTORY OF AFFINITY DIAGRAMS
Affinity diagrams were created in the 1950s by Japanese anthropologist Jiro Kawakita It is sometimes called the K-J Method. Jiro Kawakita worked in remote Nepalese villages researching problems, related to water supplies and transportation. He was awarded the Ramon Magsaysay Award in 1984.

Affinity diagrams were part of the Seven Management and Planning Tools, used in Total Quality Control in Japan.

Jiro Kawakita named the method around 1967 and published a comprehensive description of the KJ method in 1986. Since 1969, Kawakita has presented KJ method workshops in Japan.

WHEN SHOULD WE USE AFFINITY DIAGRAMS?

An Affinity Diagram is useful when you want to:

1. Make sense out of large volumes of chaotic data.
2. Encourage new patterns of thinking. An affinity diagram can break through traditional or entrenched thinking.

STRENGTHS

1. It is a simple method.
2. Supports innovation.
3. Causes breakthroughs to emerge
4. Helps groups come to a consensus about most important issues
5. Multiple people can combine their ideas by on post-it notes and be organizing them.
6. Organizing generates useful discussions.
7. Builds critical thinking skills.
8. Allows for involvement of each team member
9. Helps your team to see the big picture and where the biggest problems are.
10. Post-it notes are a flexible method to organize ideas into various levels of groups and sub-groups.
11. It is both a creative and analytical method
12. Promotes the emergence of breakthrough thinking
13. Most effective when applied to a team with varied perspectives and open-mindedness.
14. Is useful to make sense of complex apparently unrelated ambiguous or chaotic data
15. It makes your analysis highly visible to others in the company.

WEAKNESSES

1. Good facilitation is required to when there is a lot of data.
2. Affinity diagrams are not portable or mobile.
3. Affinity diagrams occupy a large space for a period.
4. Can be time-consuming when there are a large number of pieces of data.
5. The small size of post-it notes and the effort of writing forces you to be brief,
6. It is an analog or physical activity
7. the rationale behind particular groupings can be lost.
8. Affinity diagrams are temporary and must be photographed to keep a permanent record.
9. It may be difficult find individual pieces of information.

USE AN AFFINITY DIAGRAM WHEN:

1. You have a large body of

information in apparent chaos.
2. To uncover hidden connections between pieces of information or ideas
3. When issues seem too broad and complex to grasp.
4. There is no clear solution evident to your team.
5. When group consensus is necessary.
6. You wish to move beyond habitual thinking and preconceived categories.
7. When other solutions to a problem have failed.
8. To rethink how issues are connected.
9. To brainstorm root causes and solutions to problems, especially when little or no data is available
10. Organize qualitative data from stakeholders to uncover insights and themes
11. The solution requires consensus amongst the team members to work effectively
12. Extract requirements from user research
13. To organize ideas from brainstorming.
14. To brainstorm root causes of problems, especially when data is confusing or ambiguous.

DO NOT USE AN AFFINITY DIAGRAM WHEN
if less than 15 items of data.

PROCESS
SELECT YOUR TEAM
Care should be taken in choosing your team. As many groups and diverse points of view involved in design delivery and use of the service as possible should be represented.
1. Keep groups to six people or less.
2. Break large groups into smaller groups of six or fewer people.
3. Have a diverse team with different genders, age, occupations and status represented.
4. Have at least two or three "T" shaped team members. That is people with two or more areas of expertise such as technology and management or administration and design. T-shaped team members make the team more flexible and help group collaboration.
5. Involve external and internal stakeholders such as customers, suppliers, internal business management, engineering, design, and sales.
6. Have customer-facing people where possible because they better see the client's perspective.

APPOINT YOUR MODERATOR
1. Create handouts with clear instructions
2. Provide copies of research summaries
3. Take breaks every 90-minutes
4. Photograph the map as it is being built.

GATHER YOUR DATA SPREAD IT OVER A WALL

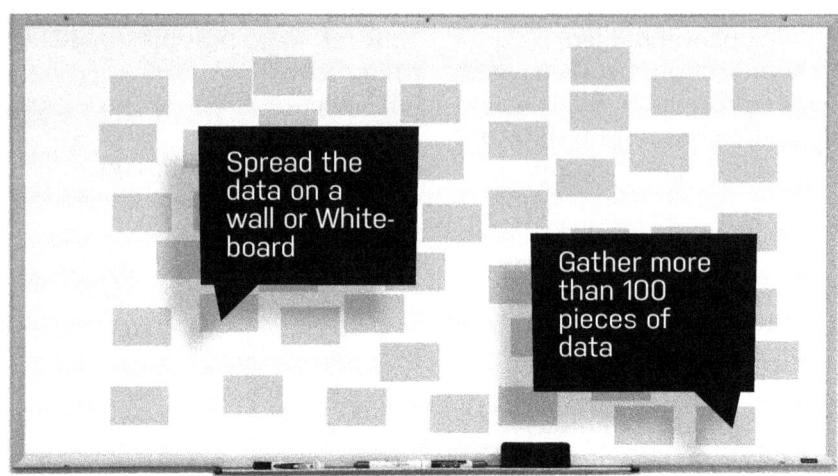

MOVE THE DATA INTO RELATED GROUPS

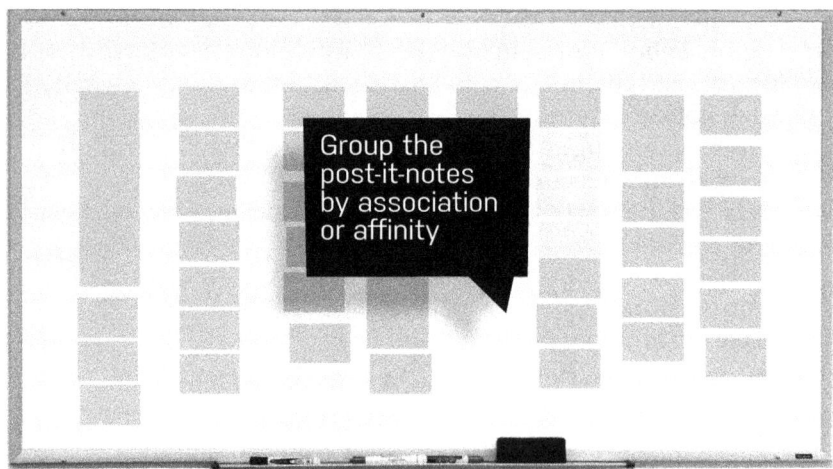

MODERATOR SKILLS
1. Effective Listening Skills
2. Flexibility
3. Customer empathy
4. Sincerely Interested in People
5. Enthusiasm
6. People management skills
7. Able to establishing common direction and buy-in.
8. Understands Group Dynamics
9. Authority
10. Neutral and Objective
11. Patient and Persistent
12. Guide discussion promptly.

RESOURCES
White-board
Large wall spaces or tables
Dry-erase markers
Sharpies
Post-it notes

There are two ways to use affinity diagrams:

RESEARCH TOOL
To make sense of a large body of research data. This approach can be used to establish connections between different pieces of research, to uncover insights from the data that can then be used to develop design concepts. With this approach, the team can develop a hierarchy of significance of the connections or themes and the insights. This hierarchy helps to establish the levels of focus for different ideas and themes uncovered by the research for the ideation design phase.

BRAINSTORMING TOOL
Affinity diagrams can also be used during the ideation or idea generation phase of a design project. When the technique is used for ideation it helps synthesize a large number of design ideas. The design team can decide which ideas are the best ideas and then combine features of various ideas to develop themes and variations through iterative cycles of brainstorming, affinity diagrams and synthesis.

GATHER YOUR DATA
First gather your data. Break the data down into pieces. For example, if an interview subject has raised several interesting points during an interview transcribe the interview, highlight the interesting points then copy each point onto a separate post-it-note. Use only one color post-it notes at this stage. The most common color used at this phase for the raw data is yellow.

FIND YOUR SPACE
Once you have selected your team, your moderator, and space to work, spread the ideas randomly across a wall, a White-board or large table. A floor in a little traffic area also can work for this stage of the process. You need plenty of space.

Affinity diagrams work best with more than 100 discrete pieces of information and work efficiently up to several thousand pieces of data.

CLUSTERING

Hand a block of blank 2" x 3" yellow post-it notes to each team member.

You can use the "Rule of 7 plus or minus 2". The summary should have no less than 5 and no more than 9 words in it, including a verb and a noun. Use also simple cartoon sketches and a combination of drawings and words. Gather your team around the place where you have placed the post-it notes. Look for ideas that seem to be related.

Go for volume, suspend judgment, build on each other's ideas and set a strict time limit. Allow 30 or 40-minutes for brainstorming ideas.

The moderator then asks the team to take two ideas that seem to belong together and place them together, at least, three feet away from the other post-it notes. Keep moving post-it notes into the groups until all the post-its have been placed into groups. It is OK to replace another person's group if it doesn't make sense to you. Some groups may have only a small number of items.

The type of relationship that you see will depend on your background, your profession your personality and your life experience.

Move related ideas into groups and continue moving the post-it notes until all notes are in groups. Some ideas may not seem to fit a group. Place those ideas into a group. If a note belongs in two groups, make a second note.

It is best that no one speaks at this stage, so different perspectives are represented.
Work silently. Ask the team to move the ideas into groups based on their gut instincts and without talking. This approach encourages unconventional thinking and discourages one person from steering the affinity. It is important to maintain silence at this stage, as it ensures that each member has an equal opportunity to apply their perspective without being influenced to conform to others' thinking.

Ask your team not to struggle over placing the data into groups, use gut instincts.
If consensus is not reached, make a duplicate of the idea and place one copy in two groups. The idea written on each post-it should be a phrase or sentence that clearly conveys the meaning to people who are not on the team. Make the notes large enough to be readable from 10 feet distance.

HEADERS

Hand out a block of blank 2" x 3" blue post-it notes to each team member. Using the second color of post-it notes, ask each participant to assign a name to each group. Write a header above each cluster that describes what connects the data in the group. Use a different color post-it notes for the headers. Blue is a color

MOVE THE DATA INTO RELATED GROUPS

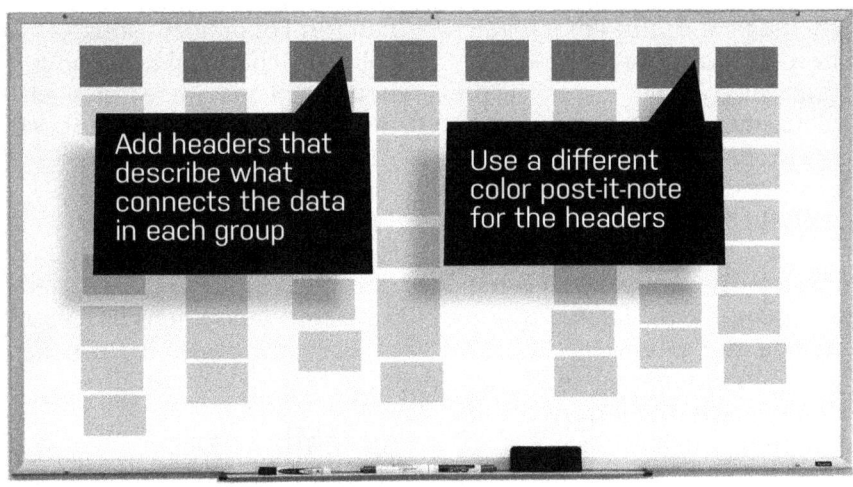

GROUP ASSOCIATED GROUPS AND SUPERGROUPS WITH HEADERS

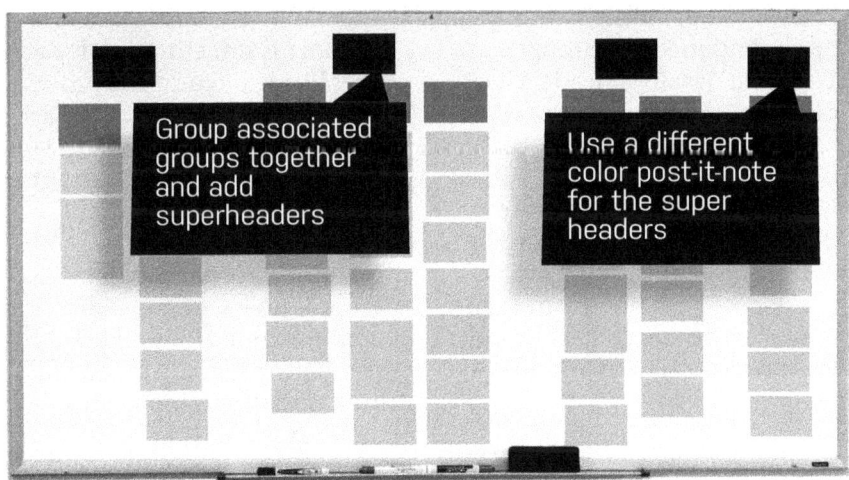

that is often used for headers. You can use any color, but it should be the same color for all headers and a different color than the color utilized in the previous phase. The most efficient use of space is to position the post-it notes in a group vertically with the header above the group.

To create headers ask for each grouping: "What key words summarize the central idea that this grouping communicates?" Sometimes a post it from within the group can be used as a header.

Create a heading for each group that captures the theme of each group. Place it above the group. A header should capture the association or affinity among the ideas contained in a group.
The team develops headers by discussing and agreeing on the wording of the header post-it notes.
Review each group and write down a name that best represents each cluster on the new set of sticky notes. Do not use full sentences for headers but summarize the association with just one or two words.

If a group has two themes, then split the group into two groups. If two groups share the same theme combine the two groups into one or move the two groups near to each other and place a header above the headers of the two groups that define the association of the two groups.

Making a simple title involves abductive thinking, which is the best form of problem-solving for complex, changing and ambiguous problems. Some notes will not fit into any group. Put these in a separate group.

When people slow down it is time to break the silence, and start discussing the groups that have emerged. When consensus is reached, move on to the next step.

SUPERHEADERS
If two groups have the same theme then place an additional header in a third color above those two groups. Leave the previous headers in place. Pink is commonly used for a combined header of two groups. This type of header is sometimes called a super header. Repeat the process until the number of groupings is between 5 and 9 groups. Ask each participant to read through the post-it notes in each group.

The moderator should then say "We will now see if we can combine some groups. Please nominate two groups that you think we can combine. Only combine groups that have the same theme but not groups that are subsets of one another"

DOT VOTING
Give each participant 3 adhesive dots and ask them to place the dots next to the header of the three groups that they think are most important in relation to the

design goals.
1. What are the user needs?
2. What are the needs of the business?
3. What technologies are most appropriate?

After each person has voted tally the number of votes for each group.

This gives you a hierarchy of importance for the themes in order to address these themes in the next phase of the design process, the ideation phase.

This is a way of efficiently selecting from a large number of ideas the preferred ideas to carry forward in the design process.

WHY USE DOT VOTING?
It is a method of selecting a favored idea by collective rather than individual judgment. It is a fast method that allows a design to progress. It leverages the strengths of diverse team member viewpoints and experiences

CHALLENGES
1. The assessment is subjective.
2. Group-think
3. Not enough good ideas
4. Inhibition
5. Lack of critical thinking

HOW
1. Gather your team of 4 to 12 participants.
2. Brainstorm ideas, for example, ask each team member to generate ten ideas as sketches.
3. Each idea should be presented on one post-it-note or page.
4. Each designer should quickly explain each idea to the group before the group votes.
5. Spread the ideas on a wall or table.
6. Ask the team to vote on their two or three favorite ideas and total the votes. You can use sticky dots or colored pins to indicate a vote or a moderator can tally the scores.
7. Rearrange the ideas so that the ideas with the dots are ranked from most dots to least.
8. Refine the preferred ideas.

AFFINITY DIAGRAM EXERCISE

WHAT IS AN AFFINITY DIAGRAM?

An affinity diagram is a method of brainstorming, in which

seemingly random ideas or suggestions are eventually organized within natural groupings.

WHY USE AN AFFINITY DIAGRAM?

1. Affinity diagrams are a great way to make sense of a large volume of chaotic information that might otherwise seem overwhelming.
2. Affinity diagrams also allow a group to see connections in ways that might not seem obvious at first.
3. Affinity diagrams can help groups reach consensus.
4. Affinity diagrams can also help team members to build upon each other's knowledge.
5. Each member of a team can contribute.
6. An affinity diagram can have anywhere from 50 to 1000 ideas many ideas may be combined with one another if they're similar, or discarded.

TIMING

Anticipate the process taking between 409 minutes and one hour to the stage of clustering ideas and associating headers.

MATERIALS

Two pads of sticky notes in three colors. One color can be used for ideas, while other can be used for the titles of the groups.

RULES

1. Go for quantity quantity breeds quality.
2. Withhold criticism for a later 'critical stage' of the process.
3. Welcome wild ideas. Wild ideas are encouraged.
4. Combine and improve ideas.

PROCESS

1. Select a target user group and a need or problem they have to solve.
2. State the problem in the form of a need statement xxxx needs to solve xxxx because xxxx.
3. Divide your team into groups of 4 to 8 people and generate possible solutions to the needs statement.
4. Record the ideas, suggestions, and opinions of each team member on sticky notes. Team members should only write one idea/suggestion/opinion per sticky note and should be encouraged to create at least five sticky notes.
5. Post everyone's sticky notes on a wall
6. Ask all team members to come to the wall and quietly look for ideas/suggestions/opinions that seem to be related
7. Ask team members to sort the related sticky notes into

groups
8. Ask a team member to write the titles of each group on different colored sticky notes, which will be the team's Affinity Diagram Titles.
9. Give everyone three votes and vote on the best idea.

VOTE FOR PREFERRED GROUPS

Each team member is given 3 votes

Give each team member some sticky dots. To create a hierarchy of what your team thinks is the hierarchy of importance of the clusters to your project give each team member three votes. This will allow you to select just one or several clusters to carry forward for further discussion or prototyping. Some companies give more senior team members more votes. For example the CEO might get six votes and an intern three. AA fast way of voting is for the moderator to go through the clusters one at a time and team members to vote by holding up their hand and the moderator puts a mark next to each group for each vote using white board markers or on a sticky note next to each group.

GLOSSARY

GLOSSARY

In this short glossary I have brought together a collection of terms used in Design Thinking, service design and user-centered design.

These fields are emerging areas of design and I believe will become the most significant areas of design this century. There are many terms that are used and these terms are still evolving.

At the back of this work you will find a list of my other publications if you would like more in-depth information about any of these fields.

I hope that you will find this collection useful.

A-B TEST
Testing technique where a percentage of site visitors are shown an alternate version of a design. The effectiveness of the two designs is then compared.

ACTOR
A person involved in the creation, delivery, support, or use of a service.

AFFINITY DIAGRAM
A tool used to organize a large number of ideas, sorting them into groups based on their natural relationships, for review and analysis

AFFORDANCES
The qualities of a design or material that affects or suggests how it can be used. For example, the affordances of a hammer (weight, handle and and grip, scribed head, etc) suggest it should be used for striking objects. Looking at affordances is especially useful when analyzing how designs or materials prompt certain behaviors. (eg. "When all you have is a hammer, everything looks like a nail."
Source dSchool Stanford

ANALOGOUS SITUATIONS
An analogous situation is a situation from another area or industry that may relate to an area of focus for a design and may suggests ways to improve it.

ANALYTIC INDUCTION
A qualitative research method that begins with a rough hypothesis, which is modified through the examination of cases that don't fit the hypothesis.

ANALYTICS
A broad term that encompasses a variety of tools, techniques and processes used for extracting useful information or meaningful patterns from data.

ARTIFACTS
Physical service touchpoints. For example the New York Underground map

BACKSTAGE/ BACKOFFICE
Backstage activities are those taken by the service delivering company employees that are not visible to the customer. Backstage actions are actions that impact customers.

Backstage actions are separated from onstage service delivery by the line of visibility. Activities above the line of visibility are seen by the client while everything below it is invisible. On an aircraft, the taking of an order for a meal is an onstage or front-stage action, and the preparation of the food is a backstage action if it is not seen by the traveler.

BETA LAUNCH
The limited launch of a software product with the goal of finding bugs before final launch.

BIAS
A one-sided viewpoint, inclination or a partial perspective. An interviewer might inadvertently bias an interviewee's answers by asking a "loaded" question, in which a desired answer is presupposed in the question.

BODYSTORMING
Prototyping method,
Service situations are be acted out,for example for example at the hotel reception. The design team cast the roles, practice the situation. often with the input of end users The purpose is to prototype and test interactions to better understand and refine them.

BRAINSTORMING
Brainstorming is a group or individual creativity approach where design solutions are generated by members of the team in a collaborative session.

A method for generating ideas, intended to inspire the free-flowing sharing of thoughts of an individual or a group of people, typically while withholding criticism in order to promote uninhibited thinking.

CARD SORTING
A technique using either cards or software, whereby users generate an information hierarchy that can then form the basis of an information architecture or navigation menu.

A technique to investigate how users tend to group. The users are given a set of cards containing individual item names and are told to sort them into related piles and label the groups. Card sorting provides insight into the user's mental model and suggests the structure and placement of items on a Website.
Source: Human Factors International

CAUSATION
A relationship between an event (the cause) and a second event (the effect), where the second event is a consequence of the first event.
Source: Human Factors International

CHANNEL
A medium for communication or delivery. Most services use more than one channel. For example phone, email, in-store or website.

CLOSED QUESTIONS
Questions that elicit a yes/no response.

CO-DESIGN
Process in which the design team directly engages end users to assist in the design to access knowledge that is crucial to develop successful design solutions.

The designers should provide ways for people to engage with each other as well as instruments to communicate, be creative, share insights and envision their own ideas. The co-design activities can support different levels of participation, from situation in which the external figures are involved just in specific moments to situations in which they take part to the entire process, building up the service together with the designers.

COGNITIVE DISSONANCE
Cognitive dissonance refers to the discomfort caused by holding two or more conflicting (dissonant) beliefs at the same time. People seek to reduce the discomfort by changing one of the beliefs, thus returning to a state of 'consonance'. So, for example, someone holding the belief that "I am a smart consumer," may be faced with the dawning realization that "I paid too much for that car." The two beliefs are in conflict (dissonant) and therefore uncomfortable, so one of the beliefs must change. To avoid undermining positive self-belief, and because it is difficult to get a different car, the user's attitude about the car will change, so that it is seen as more valuable, and therefore worth the price paid.
Source: Human Factors International

COMPARISON TESTS Usability test that compares two or more designs. Examples might be comparing alternative wireframes, comparing before and after designs, or a comparing a design against competitor designs.
Source: Human Factors International

CONCEPTUAL MODEL
A model constructed by the users in their mind to understand the working or the structure of objects, based on their mental model and previous experience, to speed up their understanding. Also called mental model.
Source: Human Factors International

CONFIRMATION BIAS
The tendency to search for, notice, and interpret information in a way that confirms one's beliefs or opinions.
Source: Human Factors International

CONTEXTUAL INQUIRY
A semi-structured field interviewing method based on a set of principles that allow it to be molded to different situations. This technique is generally used at the beginning of the design process and is good for getting rich information, but can be complex and time-consuming.

CODE
a word chosen to represent an idea, topic, or event that is an important theme of the interviews. After these words are decided on, they are connected to colors or symbols used to mark passages of the transcripts.

CODING
The process of marking passages of the interview's transcript that are about the same thing. By same thing we mean-the passages have the same phrases repeated in them or they talk about the topic in the same way. These passages are marked with a name,the code, which is usually connected to a longer explanation of what the

passages have in common. Codes stress what themes run through the interview or the collection of interviews.

COLLABORATIVE DESIGN
Inviting input from users, stakeholders and other project members.

COLLECTIVE INTELLIGENCE
Collective intelligence is shared knowledge that comes from the collaboration of a group of people and is expressed in consensus decisio-making. Collective intelligence requires openness, sharing ideas, experiences and perspectives.

CONTEXT
Context
The world the service belongs to. The context is the specific frame in which the service takes place. Exploring and defining the context means setting the project boundaries in terms of limits but also opportunities. Context is external elements that surround and influence design. These items can be physical and non-physical and cultural. The environmental context relates to the time, the day, the location, the type of place and any other physical aspect that could influence your design. The surrounding context influences the success of design.

CONTEXTUAL INQUIRY
Interviewing users in the location that they use the product or service, to understand their tasks and challenges.

CONVERGENT
Process of Narrowing down ideas through synthesis.

CROSS-DISCIPLINARY COLLABORATION
Combines the wisdom and skills of different professional disciplines working in close and flexible collaboration. Each team member requires disciplinary empathy allowing them to work collaboratively with other discipline members. Design teams can include anthropologists, engineers, educators, doctors, lawyers, scientists, etc. in the innovative problem-solving process.

CULTURAL PROBE
Cultural probes are sets of simple artifacts (such as maps, postcards, cameras, or diaries) that are given to users for them to record specific events, feelings or interactions in their usual environment, in order to get to know them and their culture better. Cultural probes are used to uncover aspects of culture and human interaction like emotions, values, connections, and trust.

CUSTOMER JOURNEY
The customer journey is a graphical representation of how the customer perceives and experiences the service interface over time It often also shows the phases before and after the interaction with the service. A customer journey map is a tool to explore, visualize, understand and refine an end user experience.

DECOY STRATEGY
A PET technique in changing impression linked to the Contrast Principle. People want to compare things before making decisions and like to make easy comparisons. So you can persuade them to select one of a small number of easily compared choices by introducing another choice that can't easily be compared. For example,

you are more likely to get people to purchase a front loader washing machine, if you give them two front loader choices (easily compared) by contrast to a third choice of a top-loader (less easy to compare). In another example, you can increase sales of an item, by offering a similar, but inferior item at about the same price. It's easy to compare them, recognize the contrast in quality, and conclude that the better quality item represents
exceptional value.
Source: Human Factors International

DEDUCTIVE ANALYSIS
A type of analysis that begins with theoretically derived hypotheses then tests them with data that were collected in accordance with the theoretical context.

DIARY STUDY
Asking users to record their experiences and thoughts about a product or task in a journal over a set period of time.

DIVERGENT
Expansive idea generation and exploration of ideas.

EMPATHIZE
This term is sometimes used to encompass the Understand and Observe steps or as a replacement for them. The use of this emotional term helps remind designers that they must always consider the human experience of real people. It's more than just seeing it from their perspectives, it's about understanding how they feel about it all and what it means to them.
Source: dSchool Stanford

EMPATHY
Principle in the Design Thinking process and human- centered design, in which the user's perspective is always represented.
Source: Libraries Toolkit

ENTRY POINTS
Position of access to a service, where people are able to engage the service as customers, providers, or stakeholders.

ETHNOGRAPHY
The process of gathering information about users and tasks directly from users in their normal work, home or leisure environment.

EVIDENCE
Service evidences are touch-points that represent parts of a service experience.

EVIDENCE-BASED DESIGN
Evidence-based design is the approach of basing design decisions on credible research to achieve the best possible outcomes. Evidence-based design emphasizes the importance of basing decisions on the best possible data for the best possible outcomes. The design is not based just on the designer's opinion.

EXPERIENCE DESIGN
The application of design processes with the goal of creating an appropriate experience for the person interacting with the
product. This process begins with understanding the needs
and wants of the user. Analysis focuses on cognitive,
emotional and motor aspects of the interaction and is
completed when the quality of the experience is measured
with the developed product.

Source: Human Factors International

EXPERIENCE PROTOTYPING
Service experiences have components that are intangible, and change over time and have multiple touch-points. Services are prototyped different ways then physical products.
Experience Prototype is a representation, that
is designed to help us understand, explore or communicate what it feels like to engage with a product, space service or system.

EXIT POINTS
Point of disengagement of a service, by stakeholders.

EXTREME USER
A person who lies at the periphery of a group of users. Extremes can can include age, ability, occupation, experience, etc. Rather than designing for a composite or "average" user, a design team will oftentimes look to extreme users for surprising and actionable insights. Focusing on extreme users can lead to more innovative solutions, more profound insights about a group of users, and new, untapped markets for a product or service.
Source: dSchool Stanford

FIELD STUDY
A field study is a general method for collecting data about users, user needs, and product requirements that involves observation and interviewing. Data are collected about task flows, inefficiencies, and the organizational and physical environments of users.

FIVE WHYS
An analysis method used to uncover the root cause of a problem.

Example of the method:
A patient had the wrong leg amputated
1. Why: Patient gave consent for amputation the night before the proposed surgery to Registrar (who was not going to undertake procedure).
2. Why: Amputation site marked with a biro (wrong leg).
3. Why: Registrar unaware of hospital policy on amputation sites being marked with a skin pencil and with bodily part being fully visible to Doctor.
4. Why: The department had no induction procedures for new medical staff working in the department.
5. Why: Because "we've never been asked to".

Root Cause Analysis Tool Kit. NHS

FOCUS GROUPS
A direct data gathering method in which a small group (8–10) of participants are led in a semi-structured, brainstorming session to elicit rapid feedback

FORMATIVE EVALUATION
Formative evaluation is a type of usability evaluation that helps to 'form' the design for a product or service. Formative evaluations involve evaluating a product or service during development, often iteratively, with the goal of detecting and eliminating usability problems.

FREE LISTING
Free listing is a technique for gathering data about a specific domain or topic by asking people to list all the items they can think of that relate to the topic. It can be used to gather data in large group settings or in one-on-one interviews.

FRONTSTAGE/FRONTOFFICE
These are face-to-face between customers and employees. These are separated from the customer by the line of interaction.

GAMBLER'S FALLACY
The mistaken belief that if an event has occurred more frequently than normal, it will happen less frequently in the future, and vice-versa.
Source: Human Factors International

GAP ANALYSIS
A technique used to determine the difference between a desired state and an actual state, often used in branding and marketing. Gap analysis may address performance issues or perception issues.
Source: Human Factors International

GESTALT PRINCIPLES
Set of principles developed by the Gestalt Psychology Movement that established rules governing how humans perceive order in a complex field of objects. Gestalt principles of visual organization state that objects near each other, with same background, connected to each other, or having similar appearance are perceived as belonging to a group.
Source: Human Factors International

GROUNDED THEORY
A qualitative research method in which theory is developed after data has been gathered and analyzed.

GROUPTHINK
Groupthink is consensus of opinion without critical reasoning or evaluation of consequences or alternatives. Employees may self-censor themselves for fear of upsetting the status quo.

HCI
Human Computer Interaction involves the study, planning, and design of the interaction between people (users) and computers.

HEURISTICS
Best practices, principles, or rules of thumb. Established principles of design and best practices in interface design, used as a method of solving usability problems by using rules of thumb acquired from human factors experience.
Source: Human Factors International

HEURISTIC EVALUATION A usability evaluation method in which one or more reviewers, preferably experts, compare a software, documentation, or hardware product to a list of design principles, referred to as heuristics and identify where the product does not follow those principles. Evaluating a website or product and documenting usability flaws and other areas for improvement.

HICK-HYMAN LAW Demonstrates the relationship between the time it takes someone to make a decision and the number of possible choices he or she has. More choices will increase decision time.
Source: Human Factors International

HIGH-FIDELITY PROTOTYPE
A prototype which is quite close to the final product, with lots of detail and a good indication of the final proposed aesthetics and functionality.

HORIZONTAL PROTOTYPE
Prototypes that display a wide range of features without fully implementing all of them. Horizontal prototypes provide insights into users' understanding of relationships across a range of features.
Source: Human Factors International

HOW MIGHT WE?
A positive, actionable question that frames the challenge but does not point to any one solution.
Source: Libraries Toolkit

HUMAN-CENTERED
An approach to design that adapts the solution to the end user through understanding the end user. The understanding is developed through engaging the end user and testing a variety of possible solutions through an iterative design process.

INDUCTIVE ANALYSIS
A type of analysis that begins with collecting and analyzing data, after which hypotheses are made.

Putting the user and user's perspective at the center of a solution. Human-centered or people-centric design requires having empathy with the user to solve for their specific needs. This philosophy involves starting with people and desirability first, before moving on to feasibility and viability.
Source: Libraries Toolkit

INTERACTION DESIGN (IXD)
Sometimes referred to as IxD, interaction design strives to create meaningful relationships between people and the products and services that they use.

INSIGHTS
Ideas or notions expressed as succinct statements that interpret patterns in your research and can provide new understanding or perspective on the issue.
Source: Libraries Toolkit

INTERCEPT
Spontaneous, casual and brief conversations with users in a natural context. Unplanned interviews that garner live feedback for your mini-pilot.
Source: Libraries toolkit

INTERVIEW GUIDE
A list of questions to direct conversation and make sure key issues get discussed. The guide should be flexible to move with conversation but at the same time its main purpose is to keep the interview on topic.

INTERVIEWER BIAS
the influence of the interviewer on the interviewee, which affects responses

I-SHAPED PERSON
Someone who has deep skills and knowledge in one area but not a broad competency across other areas.

ITERATIVE CONSULTATIVE PROCESS
An iterative consultative process is a design process of inviting diverse stakeholders to review a design and give feedback in order to improve the design from their point of view.

ITERATE
The act of repeating a process with the aim of approaching a desired goal, target or result. Each repetition of the process is also called an iteration. In Design Thinking it refers to the cycles of prototyping, testing and revision.

ITERATIVE DESIGN PROCESS
Iterative design is the process of prototyping testing and refining a design in a series of repeated steps.

JOURNEY MAP
A visual representation of a particular person or persona's experience with a service. The experience is documented over time and often shows multiple channels.

LEADING QUESTION
a question that is phrased in a way that suggests to the interviewee an answer that the researcher prefers.

LEARNINGS
The most basic level of information you record from your research, including direct quotes, anecdotes, first impressions, notes on the environment, notes on what was most memorable or surprising, and more.
Source: Libraries Toolkit

LIKERT SCALE
A type of survey question where respondents are asked to rate the level on which they agree or disagree with a given statement on a numeric scale, e.g., 1–7, where 1 = strongly agree and 7 = strongly disagree. (Also see Rating Scale.)
Source: Human Factors International

LINE OF VISIBILITY
In a service blueprint this is a line that separates face to face customer employee interactions from customer employee interactions that are remote or not face to face.

LOADED WORD
a word that has positive or negative connotations and can influence the interviewee's response to a question.

LOW-FIDELITY PROTOTYPE
A quick and easy translation of high-level design concepts into tangible and testable artifacts, giving an indication of the direction that the product is heading. Prototypes that are simple, focused on one or two features. Low resolution prototyping allows a team to make their ideas tangible and gather feedback.

MASLOW'S HIERARCHY OF NEEDS
A theory of motivation, in which individuals' needs are described as a hierarchy, often illustrated as layers in a pyramid. Needs at each level must be met prior to an individual aspiring to the next level. Maslow's theory describes five levels: Physiological, Safety, Social, Esteem and Self-actualization. In PET we can design to meet needs at one or more of these levels. For example, a mobile phone may meet people's safety ('I need to contact you in an emergency'), social ('I like to keep in touch wherever I am') and self-esteem needs ('Look at my cool phone'), with somewhat different design considerations applying to each of these levels.
Source: Human Factors International

MINIMUM VIABLE PRODUCT
A minimum viable product is a simple version of a new product which allows a team to learn the maximum amount about customers with the least effort.
The goal of an MVP is to test fundamental business hypotheses as efficiently in the real-world as possible.

MODERATOR
A person that works with a group to regulate, but not lead, a discussion. Whereas a facilitator might take charge of a discussion to shepherd it in a specific direction, a moderator remains passive, without explicitly leading the process or driving a desired outcome. A moderator takes the lead from the participants, listening and intervening only when necessary to encourage further discussion or ask for clarity for other participants or audiences.

NEEDS
A necessary function or condition. There are a wide variety of human needs such as food, shelter, security, affection and self fulfillment.

OUTSIDE-IN PERSPECTIVE
This is the perception that people outside of an organization have of the organization and it's products and services such as customers and other stakeholders.

PAPER PROTOTYPE
Paper prototyping is the process of creating rough, often hand-sketched, drawings of a user interface, and using them in a usability test to gather feedback. A rough, often hand-sketched, drawing of a user interface, used in a usability test to gather feedback. Participants point to locations on the page that they would click, and screens are manually presented to the user based on the interactions they indicate.

PARADOX OF CHOICE
Limiting choice is a PET technique in changing impression. Paradoxically, people think they want many choices, but can, in fact, be overwhelmed by the complexities too many choices introduce to decision-making. So, people are more likely to be persuaded to make a purchase (or other decision) if you limit their choice to a small number, often no more than three or four.
Source: Human Factors International

PARTICIPATORY DESIGN
An approach that involves stakeholders such as clients, end users, community members in the design process to ensure that the design meets the needs of those it is serving as well as generating buy-in. A type of social research in which the people being studied have significant control over and participation in the research.

PERSONA
A persona is a fictitious identity that reflects one of the user groups for who you are designing. A representation of a user segment with shared needs and characteristics. In user-centered design and marketing, personas are archetypal characters that represent different user segments that might use a product or service in a similar way.

PLACEBO EFFECT
A PET technique in changing impression. In medicine, for example, you can achieve health improvements just by giving the impression you are treating patients with a drug, even if

you are giving them a 'placebo', a neutral substance with no known medical properties. There is evidence that the more expensive patients think the drug to be, the greater the placebo effect.
Source: Human Factors International

POINT OF VIEW OR POV
In Design Thinking, a POV means the point of view of a very particular person. Creating a point of view involves synthesizing the data gained in the Understand and Observe phases in order to create a common reference/inspiration for later ideation and prototyping. The idea is to focus on a real person, with many of the concrete details found during the Understand/Observe phases. One approach is to develop one or two concise sentences that express User+Need+Insight.
Good: "Mark is a shy, recent college graduate who needs a way to stay connected with the college community because he feels that his life could be more exciting. Alumni newsletters and college reunions need not apply."
Bad:"Mark needs a website to share pictures and news with the people he met in college because he feels lonely."
Source: dSchool Stanford

POWER OF EXPECTATION
A PET technique in changing impression. Presenting goods or services in a way that raises the expectation that they will be good, results in users perceiving them as better. A wellformatted report, for example will be seen as better written than a scruffy one, even if the text is exactly the same. Similarly, a well presented meal will not only be more tempting than the same food just thrown on the plate, but will also taste better (as every good chef knows!). So, in PET, if we design to give the expectation that goods and services will be good, they are more likely to be experienced as good.
Source: Human Factors International

PROBES
Areas you want to go more in-depth in an interview.

A technique used during in-depth interviews to explore the interviewee's emotions about the topic we're researching. The 'probing' questions asked gently nudge the interviewees to disclose their feelings and beliefs. For example: "How do you feel about shopping online?"
Source: Human Factors International

PROTOTYPE
A prototype is a model built to test a concept with end users in order to learn from. Prototyping helps understand real, working conditions rather than a theoretical conditions.

QUESTIONNAIRES
A research instrument consisting of a series of questions and other prompts for the purpose of gathering information from respondents.

REFRAMING
Reframe to create different perspectives and new ideas.

How to reframe:
1. Define the problem that you would like to address.
2. There is more than one way of looking at a problem. You could also define this problem in

another way as."
3. What if a male or female used it?
4. What if it was used in China or Argentina?
5. "The underlying reason for the problem is."
6. "I think that the best solution is."
7. "You could compare this problem to the problem of."
8. "Another, different way of thinking about it

RETURN ON INVESTMENT (ROI)
A monetary evaluation of benefits relative to the effort or expenditure invested; a measure of how much return, usually measured as profit or cost savings, results from a given use of money. In the context of usability, ROI is the monetary (or other) benefit gained as a result of an investment in good usability design.
Source: Human Factors International

REVERSE CARD SORT
A usability testing technique, opposite to that of a card sort, where participants are given a list of items to see if they can figure out where to find them. Their success validates the self evidence of the navigational structure of a design. Categories have already been made and labeled appropriately
Source: Human Factors International

ROLE-PLAY
Assign roles and act out scenarios with props and end users feedback to refine your design.

SATISFACTION SYSTEM
The satisfaction system is the system of how the products or services satisfy the customer's needs. It includes the product or service and its related products or service. It involves understanding how related products add value to the main product. Customers are interested in the entire system beyond the individual product.

RULE OF RECIPROCATION
The technique is built on a social rule where people given a gift feel compelled to give something back. For example: You give your customer a small gift. Later, they're likely to consider signing up for your new service.
Source: Human Factors International

SCALE
Service design considers micro and macro scales ,detailed interactions, and holistic overviews of an experience.

SCENARIOS
A scenario is a hypothetical narrative illustrating an event or series of events. It is a method of imagining a user experience in the real-world.

Use scenarios are a method of prototyping ideas in order to explore and refine them. Scenarios are short stories about people and activities that describe typical usage and focus on goals, actions and objects. Scenarios evoke reflection in design and provide a common reference point. Scenarios help express the requirements of the different stakeholders in a format that can be understood by the other stakeholders. They can be written, illustrated, acted or filmed. Scenario generating aims to predict how people could act in particular situations.

A concrete, often narrative, description of a user performing tasks in a specific context sufficiently detailed that design implications can be inferred.
Source: Human Factors International

SENSORIAL DESIGN
Sensorial Design is a term used to include the presentation of an experience in all senses. For example, Visual Design only covers visual expression and presentation to the visual sense. Audio Design includes the creation of music, sound effects, and vocals to communicate and entertain in the aural sense (hearing). Likewise, all of the other human senses (touch, smell, taste, etc.) are elements of an experience that can be designed.

SERVICE DESIGN
Design for experiences that reach people through many
different touch-points, and that happen over time.
British Standard for Service Design: BS 7000 -3, BS 7000 -10, BS EN ISO 9000

Service designs can be both tangible and intangible. Service design can involve artifacts, communication, context and behaviors. It
should be consistent, easy to use and have the strategic alliance.

Gillian Hollins, Bill Hollins, Total Design: Managing The Design Process in the Service Sector

SERVICE ECOLOGY
A service ecology is a system of people, objects and the relationships between them that form a service.

System in which the service is integrated: i.e. a holistic visualization of the service system. All the factors are gathered, analyzed and visualized: politics, the economy, employees, law, societal trends, and technological development. The service ecology is thereby rendered, along with its attendant agents, processes, and relations. *Mager 2009*

Ultimately, sustainable service ecologies depend on
a balance where the actors involved exchange value
in ways that is mutually beneficial over time.
Live|work 2008

SENSUALIZATION
Sensualization is the approach of considering the experience to be the total of the individual experiences of the five senses.

SERVICE
An exchange of value, involving tangible and intangible elements A system of products spaces human interactions and experiences.

SERVICE MOMENTS
Discrete points of interaction between a user and a service, often mapped out in a user journey. An example of a service moment is a patron placing a hold on a book, which can be done at home via the website, in the library via the website, or at the reference desk.
Source: Libraries Toolkit

SERVICE SYSTEM
The ecology of relationships, interactions, and contexts of a service. channels, resources, and touchpoints, internal and external, that facilitate the delivering of a

service.

STAKEHOLDER
A person, group, or organization directly or indirectly involved or affected by a product, service or experience.

Stakeholders include any individuals who are influence by the design. Specifically, the project team, end users, strategic partners, customers, alliances, vendors and senior management are project stakeholders

Possible stakeholders
1. Employees
2. Shareholders
3. Government
4. Customers
5. Suppliers
6. Prospective employees
7. Local communities
8. Global Community
9. Schools
10. Future generations
11. Ex-employees
12. Creditors
13. Professional associations
14. Competitors
15. Investors
16. Prospective customers
17. Communities

Why involve stakeholders?
1. Stakeholder analysis helps to identify:
2. Stakeholder interests
3. Ways to influence other stakeholders
4. Risks
5. Key people to be informed during the project
6. Negative stakeholders as well as their adverse effects on the project

SWIMLANES
An approach used in service design involving arranging descriptive boxes into rows (the "swim lanes") to provide additional context about how the steps are related. Work flow is represented over time and is usually read from left to right.

SYNTHESIS
The sense-making process in which research is translated and interpreted into insights that prompt design. Useful frameworks for synthesis include journeys, Venn diagrams, two by twos and maps.
Source: Libraries Toolkit

STAKEHOLDER MAP
A visual representation of the stakeholders in a service and the relationships between them.

SERVICE DESIGN
Service design is a form of conceptual design which involves the activity of planning and organizing people, infrastructure, communication and material components of a service in order to improve its quality and the interaction between service provider and customers.
Service design - Wikipedia, the free encyclopedia, https://en.wikipedia.org/wiki/Service_design (accessed March 20, 2016).

SOCIAL DESIGN
Design done for the social good or top positively impact society.

STRATEGIC DESIGN
Design that focuses on big picture systematic problems in order to increase an organization's future innovative and competitive advantage.

STORYBOARD
A storyboard is a graphic sequence

of illustrations, words or images for the purpose of communicating a user scenario or experience. Storyboarding, was developed at Walt Disney during the early 1930s. A storyboard is a tool inspired by the film-making industry, where a visual sequence of events is used to capture a user's interactions. Depending on the audience, it may be an extremely rough sketch, purely for crystallizing your own ideas.

SUMMATIVE TESTING Testing done to measure the success of the design in terms of human performance and preference.
Source: Human Factors International

THINK-ALOUD PROTOCOL
A direct observation method of user testing that involves asking users to think out loud as they are performing a task. Users are asked to say whatever they are looking at, thinking, doing, and feeling at each moment. This method is especially helpful for determining users' expectations and identifying what aspects of a system are confusing.

TOUCHPOINTS
A touchpoint is any point of contact between a customer and the provider of a service, product or experience. A touchpoint is where a potential customer or customer comes in contact with your brand before, during and after a transaction.

Identifying your touchpoints is an important step toward creating a journey map or a service blueprint. Each touchpoint is an opportunity to create a better customer experience. A touchpoint can be a physical, virtual or human point of interaction. Chris Risdon from Adaptive Path defines touchpoints in this way. 'A touchpoint is a point of interaction involving a specific human need in a specific time and place.' Laura Patterson of VisionEdge defines a touchpoint as " any customer interaction or encounter that can influence the customer's perception of your product, service, or brand."

TRANSCRIPTION
The process of turning audio or video recordings into a typed format.

T-SHAPED PERSON
A person who has deep competency in a particular subject area and broad knowledge and skills across a range of disciplines.

TWO BY TWO MATRIX
A type of framework with opposing axes showing a spectrum along a particular dimension on each axis. This framework is used to organized ideas within the four quadrants, or to demonstrate mappings of ideas across several dimensions.
Source Libraries Handbook

UNIQUE SELLING PROPOSITION
An exclusive message that concisely describes a product
against its competition, and which the business or brand can use consistently in its advertising and promotion to achieve a cutting edge in the market.
Source: Human Factors International

UNMET NEEDS
Six principles that will ensure a design is compatible with user needs:
1. The design is based upon an explicit understanding of users, tasks and environments.

2. Users are involved throughout design and development.
3. The design is driven and refined by user-centered evaluation.
4. The process is iterative.
5. The design addresses the whole user experience.
6. The design team includes multidisciplinary skills and perspectives.

Some questions to ask:
1. Who are the users?
2. What are the users' tasks and goals?
3. What are the users' experience levels?
4. What functions do the users need from the design?
5. What information will be needed by end-users?,
6. In what form do they need it?
7. How do users think the design should work?

USABILITY

Is the ease of use and learning of an object, such as a book, software application, website, machine, tool or any object that a human interacts with.

USABILITY ROUND-TABLE

A meeting in which a group of end users is invited to bring
specific work samples and discuss the validity of an early
prototype.
Source: Human Factors International

USE CASES

A use case is a list of steps that define the interactions between a user and a system. Use cases, especially when used as requirements for software development, are often constructed in UML, with defined actors and roles.

USER-CENTERED DESIGN

A design process during which the needs of the user is considered at all times. Designers consider how a user is likely to use the product, and they then test the validity of their assumptions in real-world tests with actual users. Design that responds to user needs that is developed through engaging and understanding the point of view of users.

USER JOURNEY

The step by step journey that a user takes to reach their goal.

USER PROFILING

Based on research of user groups develop different character profiles to represent your users. These are also called personas.

USER VALIDATION

Process of testing to determine if the user's needs or requirements have been met

VALUE EXCHANGE

A service provider makes a promise to the service
recipient in exchange for some form of value. The movement of value from the service provider to the recipient is the value exchange.

VANITY METRICS

Data that make you feel good, but is not very useful or actionable such as new users gained per day or number of downloads. Vanity metrics do not reflect the key drivers of a business.

VERTICAL PROTOTYPE

Prototypes that display just a few complex features of a
product and almost completely implement only these

features. Vertical prototype tests provide insights into users' understanding of the complexity, issues, and problems of a specific feature.
Source: Human Factors International

VISUAL HIERARCHY
Refers to the overall page layout and its ability to lead the users' attention through the page elements. Effective visual hierarchies create an appropriate balance in composition that draws users to top levels of the hierarchy while optimizing visual access to important page level elements
Source: Human Factors International

WICKED PROBLEM
A wicked problem is a problem with contradictory, and changing requirements. The term 'wicked' is used, not in the sense of evil but rather its resistance to resolution.

Wicked problems are characterized by:
1. The solution depends on how the problem is framed.
2. Stakeholders have different world views and frames for understanding the problem.
3. The constraints of the problem and the resources needed to solve it change over time.
4. The problem is never solved definitively.

Source: Wicked problem:definition of wicked problem and synonyms http://brevard.ifas.ufl.edu/commu

WIREFRAME
A rough guide for the layout of a website or app, either done with pen and paper or with wireframing software. The wireframe depicts the page layout and shows how the elements work functionally. It focuses on what a web interface does, not what it looks like. Wireframes can be sketches or computer images.

WIZARD OF OZ
A user-based evaluation of unimplemented technology where, generally unknown to the user, a human or team is simulating some or all of the responses of the system.

WORKAROUND
A user's personal solution to a problem with a service or product, that circumvents the standard procedure. It is often temporary or makeshift. Observing these behaviors often leads to fruitful advances in insights and inspiration.
Source: Libraries Toolkit

INDEX

INDEX

Symbols

5 Whys 36
10x10 37
101 brainstorming 37
635 Method 37
.x 21, 47, 80, 92, 93, 94, 95, 96

A

abilities 46
A-B test 119
action bias 59
activities 52, 57, 74, 76, 97, 103, 120
activity 52, 56, 67, 76, 77, 91, 94, 102
Activity Map 66
actor 119
acts 11
affinity 56
affinity diagram 36, 44, 56, 105, 106, 107, 108, 109, 111, 119
affordance 119
age 16, 46, 62
Allport, Gordon 58
ambiguity bias 59
analgous situations 119
analysis 68
analytic induction 119
analytics 119
analyze 52, 57, 71, 76, 83, 97
anchoring bias 59
Annapurna 105
anthropump 4, 50
Apple 47, 155
artifact 60
artifacts 119
Artifacts 119
Ash Maurya 72, 73, 98
association 110

audio 73
Australia 155
Autodesk 147

B

backoffice 119
backstage 119
Bavelas, Alex 57, 67, 99
Becker, Ernest 50
behavior 11, 13, 50, 58, 59, 76, 82, 91, 92, 93, 94, 95, 96, 97, 102
behavioral map 4, 50, 51
behavior segmentation 46
benchmarking 4, 35, 36, 42, 45, 51, 69
benefits 51
Benefit segmentation 46
benefits map 4, 51, 70
Benefits map 4, 51, 70
Bennet 74, 77
beta launch 120
bias 4, 12, 13, 45, 59, 60, 71, 72, 73, 74, 76, 77, 80, 81, 82, 83, 89, 91, 92, 93, 94, 95, 96, 97, 120, 121, 126
blank 58, 112
block 112
Blue Ocean 36
blueprint 101-155, 133-155
body language 11, 76, 83
body storming 37
bodystorming 120
boundary 52
boundary shifting 4, 52
brainstorming 35, 37, 42, 46, 57, 105, 107, 109, 111, 112, 115, 120, 124, 154
brand 133

breaking down silos 19
British Design Council 38

C

camera 52, 53, 58, 86
camera journal 4, 36, 52
cameraman 80
Camp, Robert 51
Caracelli 84
cards 53, 54, 55, 62, 63
card sorting 37, 53, 120
causation 120
challenge 57, 73, 115
channels 100, 120, 127, 131
China 130, 155
Cisco 147
citizenship status 46
closed card sort 4, 53
closed card sorting 53, 54
closed questions 120
clustering 112
clustering insights 35
co-creation 17, 18
code 121
co-design 37, 120
coding 82, 121
cognitive dissonance 59, 121
collaboration 13, 17
collaborative 120
collaborative design 122
collective intelligence 122
color 113
combine 81
common ground 36
communities 132, 135
comparison tests 121
competitive advantage 21, 51, 132
competitive products 35
competitive strategy 51
competitors 132
complex 63, 84, 85, 105, 106, 107, 108, 109, 114, 121, 125, 134
complexity 47, 106, 107, 135
concept 52, 54, 57, 71

conceptual model 121
confirmation bias 121
conflicts of interest 60
consensus matrix 4
constraints 35, 47
context 35, 44, 46, 55, 57, 67, 68, 71, 73, 74, 75, 76, 77, 80, 81, 82, 83, 85, 86, 91, 92, 93, 94, 95, 96, 97, 98, 99, 100, 122, 123, 126, 130, 131, 132
contextual 73, 74, 75, 77, 80
contextual inquiry 5, 61, 73, 74, 75, 77, 121, 122
contextual interviews 73, 75, 80
contextual laddering 75
convergent 36, 122
conversation 73, 74, 81, 82
conversation cards 54
Cornell University 87
covert 92
covert observation 5, 92
cross-disciplinary collaboration 122
cross-disciplinary teams 16
cultural 55, 62
cultural inventory 55
cultural probe 55, 122
cultural probes 55, 122
culture 21, 35
Curedale, Rob 148, 153
curious 45
current state maps 100
customer 67, 75, 101, 133
customer experience 10, 100, 101, 133
customer journey 122
customer segments 45
customer's perspective 106

D

Dam, Rikke 102
data 52, 57, 58, 67, 71, 75, 76, 80, 83, 86, 97, 109, 110, 113
data analysis 11, 25

day experience method 56
day in the life 4, 36, 57, 78
day in the life study 4, 57, 78
DCC 147
debriefing 62
deck of cards 53, 54
decoy strategy 122
deductive analysis 123
deliverables 35
Dell 155
demographic segmentation 46
Descriptive question matrix 64, 65
desert island 36
Design Community College 2, 3, 148, 149, 150, 151, 152, 153, 154
design problem 47
design process 57, 115
design teams 155
design thinking 35
design thinking process 16, 18, 25, 35, 36, 42, 123
development process 21, 24
diagram 105, 108
diary methods 58
diary study 58, 123
differentiation 35
digital camera 58
direct observation 5, 93
disabilities 46
discovery 4, 42, 44, 45
Discovery Phase 44
Discovery Process 45
Disney method 37
divergent 123
document 35, 73
dot voting 4, 37, 57, 79, 114, 115
double diamond design process model 38

E

Edison, Thomas 15, 17
education 16, 46
Eisenhower, Dwight D. 21
E-mail 76
E-mail interview 76
emotional 62, 63
emotion cards 4, 58, 62, 63
emotions 10, 46, 62, 64, 102, 122, 129
empathy 25, 36, 46, 52, 123
employee training 37
empowered teams 16, 19
end user 45, 71, 122, 126
entry points 123
entry Points 123
ethnographic frameworks 47
ethnographic methods 50
ethnography 123
Europe 155
evaluation matrix 37
evidence 123
evidence-based design 123
exit points 124
expectations 13, 46, 133
experience 35, 46, 67, 101, 133, 155
experience design 10, 123
experience maps 36, 46
experience prototyping 124
experiences 57, 76, 82, 83
extreme user 76, 124
extreme user interview 76

F

facilitating 11, 16, 25
failure 20, 25, 44
false causality 59
feedback 42, 86
Festinger, Leon 59
field study 124
five whys 4, 63, 124
flexibility 21
fly-on-the-wall 4, 67
focus 57, 58, 67, 74, 82
Focus 153, 154
focus groups 4, 36, 44, 61, 67, 68,

124, 153, 154
follow-up sessions 50
Ford 147
formative evaluation 124
frame 73
framework 82, 133
framing bias 59
free association 36
free listing 124
frontstage 125
funding bias 60
future 100, 103

G

gain 80
gambler's fallacy 125
gap analysis 125
Gaver, Bill 55
gender 16, 35, 46
generalizability 85
generating ideas 120
geographic segmentation 46
Gestalt principles 125
glossary 119
goal 51, 54, 63, 80
Goal grid 36
goals 9, 10, 13, 35, 36, 46, 54, 60, 64, 65, 66, 71, 74, 90, 94, 95, 100, 101, 103, 115, 130, 134
Goals 61, 90
Google 54
government 45, 90, 132, 147
Graham 84
Greene 84
groan zone 40, 41
grounded theory 125
group 35, 57, 77, 80, 81, 113, 115, 155
group interview 5, 76, 77
Group interview 5, 77
groups 67, 76, 77, 80, 110, 113, 117
groupthink 57, 59, 80, 115, 125
Guba 85

guided storytelling 5, 77
Guided storytelling 5, 77
Gutman 75

H

Hamilton 155
HCI 125
headers 113
health 46
Hermagoras of Temnos 102
heuristic evaluation 125
heuristics 37, 125
Hick-Hyman Law 125
hierarchy 35, 45, 54, 111, 115, 120, 127, 135
high fidelity prototype 126
history 107
Holtzblatt 74, 77
horizontal prototype 126
how might we? 126
HP 147, 155
human-centered design 126
human factors 25, 125
human needs 67, 128

I

idea 35, 42, 57, 58, 81, 103, 115
ideation 4, 42, 68, 111, 115, 129
ideation decision matrix 4, 68
implementation 37, 42, 90, 100
impromptu interviews 80
income 46
indirect observation 5, 91, 93, 94
inductive analysis 126, 126–155
information 58, 73, 74, 75, 76, 80, 81, 103
inhibition 57, 115
innovate 21
innovation 10, 21, 22, 24, 25, 59, 105, 108, 155
Innovation 21, 36, 59
Innovation bias 59
innovation diagnostic 21
insight 52, 54, 58, 71

insights 35, 36, 51, 52, 53, 54, 57, 58, 68, 71, 73, 75, 76, 77, 81, 82, 86, 92, 93, 94, 95, 96, 97, 99, 107, 109, 111, 120, 121, 124, 126, 132, 135
intangible 124, 131
Intel 147
interact 67
interaction design 126
Interactive Design Foundation 102
intercept 126
interview consent form 87
interviewer bias 126
interview guide 4, 48, 72, 74, 81, 82, 83, 126
interviewing 4, 5, 14, 35, 36, 37, 44, 54, 55, 56, 58, 71, 72, 73, 74, 75, 76, 77, 80, 81, 82, 83, 85, 86, 98, 122
Interviewing methods 5, 74
interviews 121, 122, 124, 126, 129, 153, 153-155, 153-155, 154, 154-155, 154-155, 154-155
Intille 56
Intuit 10
intuition 106
investment 24
I-shaped person 126
iteration 42, 127
iterative consultative process 126
iterative design 127

J

Japan 105, 106, 108
Jastrow 53, 54
Jehl, Francis 17
Jonathan Ive 47
Jossey-Bass 40
journey 100, 101, 133
journey map 100, 101, 127, 133
judgment 18, 45, 57, 112, 115

K

Kaner, Sam 40, 41
Kaner,Sam 40, 41
Kawakita, Jiro 105, 106, 107, 108
key differentiation 35
key problem approach 105
Kipling, Rudyard 103
KJ method 105, 108
Krueger, Richard A. 68

L

laddering 75
language 16, 46, 148, 149, 150, 151, 152, 153, 154
launch 42
leading question 127
Likert scale 127
Lincoln 85
line of visibility 120, 127
listening 9, 13, 45
listening skills 11, 12, 14
loaded word 127
lotus blossom method 37
low fidelity prototyping 127
Luckner and Nadler 40

M

Malinowski, Bonislaw 93, 95
manager of logistics 11, 25
man in the street interview 80
manufacturing 42
mapping 50, 51, 52, 57, 66, 100, 101
mapping methods 100, 133, 150, 151
marketing 37, 90, 155
Maslow's hierarchy of needs 127
materials 42
Mead, Margaret 93, 95
meaning 10, 82, 97
Merton, Robert K 68
methods 57, 148-155
metrics 84, 90, 100, 101, 134

milestones 36
mind Maps 36
minimum viable product 128
mixed method research 83
mobile 56, 86
mobile diary study 86
mobility 46
moderator 58, 109, 115
modify 51
Monteiro, Robert A 67, 99
multidisciplinary 45, 47, 134
mystery shopper 89, 90, 91
Mystery shopper 89, 91

N

narrative 101, 130, 131
nationality 46
naturalistic group interview 80
needs 12, 35, 46, 47, 53, 57, 58, 67, 71, 74, 83, 97, 100, 103, 115, 127, 128, 133
negative stakeholders 132
Nelson, Doreen 97
Nestle 147
Ngram 54
Nielsen, Jakob 53, 54
Nietzsche, Friedrich 17
Nike 147
non-participant observation 94
non verbal 86
North America 155
notes 57, 73, 115

O

objectives 42, 92, 93, 94, 95, 96
observation 5, 36, 44, 46, 56, 57, 67, 91, 92, 93, 94, 95, 96, 97, 99, 153, 154
observation skills 11, 14
observe 35, 36, 47, 57, 67, 73, 75, 77, 81, 92, 93, 94, 96, 100, 123, 129
observer 67, 91, 92, 93, 94, 95, 96, 97

occupation 46
Olsen 75
one-on-one interview 73, 74, 75, 80, 81
open card sort 4, 53
opportunities 36, 60, 101, 112, 133
organization 21, 24
outside-in perspective 128
overt observation 95

P

pain points 100, 101
Panicucci 41
paper prototyping 37, 128
paradox of choice 128
participant observation 95
participants 11, 12, 13, 14, 50, 52, 53, 54, 55, 56, 57, 58, 61, 62, 63, 67, 68, 71, 72, 75, 76, 77, 80, 81, 82, 85, 86, 87, 89, 91, 92, 93, 94, 95, 96, 97, 99, 115, 124, 128, 130, 147
participation 14, 20, 68, 88, 105, 121, 128
participatory design 128
Patton 85
perceptual maps 36
performance 35
permission 94, 95
person 74, 81, 115
persona 36, 40, 128, 134
personal inventory 97
personas 36, 45, 50, 56
phase 115
photo elicitation interview 82
photograph 82
PICTIVE 37
placebo effect 128
planning 4, 42, 71, 106, 108
point of view 35, 36, 37, 42, 44, 45, 57, 71, 73, 75, 77, 81, 100
point of view (POV) 126, 129, 134
Post-it-Notes 112

POV 36
power of expectation 129
presentation 61
probes 129
problem 35, 103
problem definition interview 72, 97
Problem definition interview 72, 98
problems 76, 103
problem-solving 18, 106, 114, 122
problem statement 47, 63
process 16, 21, 24, 45, 52, 57, 58, 77, 82, 91, 101, 115, 120, 122, 131, 134, 148, 149
product 24, 42, 51, 73, 75, 76, 80, 81, 100, 133, 155
product design 155
project goals 36
prototype 120, 124, 126, 127, 128, 129, 134, 135
prototyping 10, 37, 42, 45, 50
psychographic segmentation 46

Q

qualitative research 21, 35, 85, 119, 125
quality 37, 108
quality assurance 37
quantitative research 21, 35, 84, 85
question guides 42
questionnaires 37, 129
questions 58, 74, 76, 77, 80, 81, 82, 83, 103

R

Radcliff-Brown, Alfred 93, 95
rearrange 58, 115
Recruitment brief 98
refine 42, 58, 76, 115
reframing 129
reframing matrix 36
relationships 73

religion 46
report writer 11, 25
reputation 91
research 5, 10, 21, 23, 35, 36, 44, 45, 46, 47, 50, 52, 54, 55, 58, 60, 61, 67, 68, 72, 73, 74, 80, 83, 84, 85, 86, 87, 90, 92, 94, 95, 97, 98, 99, 105, 107, 109, 111, 119, 123, 125, 126, 127, 128, 129, 132, 134, 153, 155
researcher 52, 53, 54, 56, 58, 63, 73, 75, 76, 77, 80, 81, 82, 83, 84, 87, 88, 91, 92, 93, 94, 95, 96, 97, 99
research goals 94, 95
research plan 4, 35, 36, 44, 47, 60
research questions 61
resources 11, 22, 24, 45, 53, 55, 57, 58, 72, 77, 97, 131, 135
return on investment (ROI) 130
reverse 130
reverse card sort 130
Reynolds 75
Riddle, Matthew 56
risks 35, 87, 95, 132
role-play 130
role playing 37, 130
Royal College of Art 55
rule of reciprocation 130

S

safety 127
Sakichi Toyoda 63
Sano 53, 54
satisfaction system 130
scale 127, 130
SCAMPER 37
scenarios 35, 37, 60, 77, 86, 130, 133
schedule 13, 35, 147
scheduler 11, 25
schools 132
scope 35

script 62, 72, 98
script for the Problem Interviews 72, 98
secondary research 35
segmentation 45, 46
segments 128
sensorial design 131
sensualization 131
service 10, 22, 24, 36, 42, 44, 45, 46, 51, 66, 67, 76, 87, 89, 90, 99, 100, 101
service blueprint 36, 101
service design 45, 130, 131, 132
service ecology 131
services 2, 6, 109, 119, 120, 122, 123, 124, 126, 127, 128, 129, 130, 131, 132, 133, 134, 135, 152, 153, 154
service safari 99
Service safari 99
service system 131
shadowing 50, 99
shareholders 132
Shoji Shiba 105
Shop-alongs 48
Siemens 147
six thinking hats 37
sketching 37, 57, 112, 115, 135
smart goals 36
social design 132
Some WWWWWH questions 103
stakeholder 21, 36, 37, 44, 45, 63, 132
stakeholders 9, 18, 21, 25, 35, 37, 42, 44, 45, 46, 47, 55, 60, 61, 102, 105, 109, 122, 123, 124, 126, 128, 130, 132, 135
Stanford University 147
status-quo bias 59
Steelcase 147, 155
STEP 76, 133
Steward, Julian Haynes 55
story 5, 73, 74, 98, 101, 102
storyboard 57

storyboarding 132, 133
storyboards 132
storytelling 77
strategic 21, 55, 59, 66
strategic design 132
strategic misrepresentation 59
strategy 14, 21, 35
strengths 108
Strickland, Rachel 97
structure 73, 75, 77, 81
structured interview 5, 81
structured observation 5
Structured observation 5, 96
style guides 37
subject 52, 71, 74, 76, 80, 82, 83, 97
subjects 52, 57, 58, 74, 81
summative testing 133
superheaders 114
suppliers 66, 132
survey 37, 55, 56
swimlane, lanes 132
SWOT analysis 45
synthesis 42, 68, 107, 111, 122, 132

T

table 57, 115
tacit knowledge 73, 75, 77, 80
Tague, Nancy R. 106
talk 76, 97
target audience 45, 46, 72, 99
tasks 51, 52, 55, 63, 73, 75, 77, 81
team 9, 10, 11, 13, 15, 16, 17, 18, 21, 25, 35, 36, 37, 44, 45, 46, 51, 55, 57, 59, 60, 63, 67, 98, 100
teams 15, 16, 18, 22, 45, 47, 105, 106, 107, 108, 109, 111, 112, 114, 115, 117, 120, 122, 124, 127, 128, 132, 134, 135, 155
technique 67, 75, 83
technologies 21
telephone 83

Telephone interview 5, 83
Teo Siang 102
Teo Siang, 102
test 119
testing 37, 42, 46, 60, 61, 72, 92, 93, 94, 96, 102
testing plan 37
themes 11, 12, 82, 85, 95, 106, 107, 109, 111, 114, 115, 122
think aloud protocol 37, 133
thinking 57, 115
time 52, 57, 58, 68, 74, 76, 80, 86, 103, 133, 155
tools 74
touch 58
touchpoints 100, 101, 119, 131, 133
Toyoda, Sakichi 63
Toyota 63
transcription 133
triangulation 84
trust 17, 89, 122
T-shaped people 126
T-shaped person 15, 16
two-by-two matrix 133

U

underlying needs 44, 45
understanding 57, 83, 97, 103
unique selling proposition 133
unmet needs 6, 22, 25, 36, 44, 45, 133
unstructured interviews 5, 83
unstructured observation 96
usability 69, 121, 134
usability study 61
use cases 134
user 115
user-centered design 119, 128, 134
user experience 46
user interviews 37
user journey 134
user needs 115

user profiling 134
users 53, 71, 73, 74, 75, 76, 77, 80, 81, 97
user stories 5, 101
user validation 134

V

value exchange 134
values 10, 44, 59, 71, 75, 97, 103, 122
vanity metrics 134
Vernile, Lucy 67, 99
vertical prototype 134
video 73, 75, 80, 81
vision 35, 42, 155
visual hierarchy 135
voting 57, 58, 79, 114, 115
VW 155

W

wall 57, 67, 110
want 74, 103
warming up exercise 36
weaknesses 108
What-How-Why 102
Whiteside, Bennet 74, 77
wicked problems 135
Williams, Anne 74
Wilmark 89
wireframing 37, 121, 135
withhold judgment 45
Wizard of Oz 37, 135
workarounds 47, 135
wrap-up 5, 73, 98
WWWWWH 36, 102, 103
WWWWWH questions 103

X

Xerox 51

07
COURSES & OTHER TITLES

DCC ONLINE COURSES
MORE INFORMATION HTTPS://DCC-EDU.ORG

OUR MISSION
Through our online programs, workshops and publications we provide skills to fulfill evolving work roles and to to create better solutions in a new economy. We provide quality education which is better value, more accessible, more flexible and more relevant for working global professionals. Online live, interactive continuing education courses that you can access from home, from work or anywhere with an internet connection.

ABOUT US
Our programs are for working designers and anyone seeking design and management training. Our online programs are presented direct from Los Angeles by some of the most experienced design professionals in the world. We offer introductory courses, five-week certificate programs and eight-week advanced certificate programs that meet once per week. The courses are delivered at a number at different times to fit your schedule and time zone. Our books have been specified as texts at many design and business schools including the University of California, Art Center Pasadena, Parsons Graduate Program, and Purdue University. We can present a custom program in your location anywhere in the world. We can tailor an online program to your schedule and needs. Contact us at info@curedale.com.

WHO HAS ATTENDED OUR COURSES?
Past participants in our on-line programs have included thousands of executives, design managers, designers from all design disciplines, architects, researchers, social scientists, engineers and other decision-makers from the following organizations including the following organizations. Tesla Motors, NASA, Kaleidoscope, Speckdesign, Intel, Nike, MillerCoors, Radiuspd, Gensler, Herman Miller,Trek bikes, Catalystnyc, Sylvania, Whipsaw, Berkeley University, Stanford University, Pininfarina, Inscape, Newbalance, MIT, Rhode Island School of Design,Tufts, Nokia, Steelcase, Mayo Clinic, Ocad, California State University Santa Barbara,University of Michigan,In Form, RIT,Honeywell, Columbia University,Nissan, Volkswagen, Sony, Nestle, Kraft Foods, Otterbox, Henry Ford Museum, Samsung, Ammunition, Siemens AG, Group, frog Design, Ziba Design, Plantronics, Luxion, Philips, Method, Visteon, Texas Instruments, Cisco, Mindspring, Hasbro, Dow Corning, Bressler Group, Reebok, Logitech, HP,CCS, Praxxis Design, Levi Strauss, NCSU, Design & Industry, Kensington, Symantec, Canberra University, Australian Government Department of Defence, Maya, Karten Design, Autodesk, Barco, Shutterstock, Lucid, Colgate, Starbucks, Sunbeam, Seimens.

OTHER TITLES
MORE INFORMATION HTTPS://DCC-EDU.ORG

DESIGN THINKING

DESIGN THINKING PROCESS AND METHODS MANUAL 4TH EDITION
Author: Robert A Curedale
Published by:
Design Community College Inc.
August 21, 2016
Paperback: 600 pages
Language: English
ISBN-10: 194080535X
ISBN-13: 978-1940805351

DESIGN THINKING PROCESS AND METHODS MANUAL 1ST EDITION
Author: Robert A Curedale
Published by:
Design Community College Inc.
Edition 1 January 2013
Paperback: 400 pages
Language: English
ISBN-10: 0988236214
ISBN-13: 978-0-9882362-1-9

DESIGN THINKING PROCESS AND METHODS MANUAL 3RD EDITION
Author: Robert A Curedale
Published by:
Design Community College Inc.
August 21, 2016
Paperback: 690 pages
Language: English
ISBN-10: 194080549X
ISBN-13: 978-1940805498

DESIGN THINKING POCKET GUIDE 2ND EDITION
Author: Curedale, Robert A
Published by:
Design Community College, Inc
Jun 01 2013
Paperback: 228 pages
ISBN-10: 098924685X
ISBN-13: 9780989246859

DESIGN THINKING PROCESS & METHODS GUIDE 2ND EDITION
Author: Curedale, Robert A
Published by:
Design Community College, Inc
January 2016
Paperback: 422 pages
Language: English
ISBN-10: 1-940805-20-1
ISBN-13: 978-1-940805-20-7

DESIGN THINKING QUICK REFERENCE GUIDE
Plastic laminated
Loose leaf one page
Author: Curedale, Robert A
Published by:
Loose Leaf: 1 pages
Publisher: Design Community College Inc.; 1st edition (2015)
ISBN-10: 194080518X
ISBN-13: 978-1940805184

DESIGN THINKING POCKET GUIDE 2ND EDITION

Author: Curedale, Robert A
Published by:
Design Community College, Inc
Jun 01 2013
Paperback: 228 pages
ISBN-10: 098924685X
ISBN-13: 9780989246859

DESIGN THINKING QUICK REFERENCE GUIDE

Plastic laminated
Loose leaf one page
Author: Curedale, Robert A
Published by:
Loose Leaf: 1 pages
Publisher: Design Community College Inc.; 1st edition (2015)
ISBN-10: 194080518X
ISBN-13: 978-1940805184

DESIGN THINKING TEMPLATES & EXERCISES

Author: Curedale, Robert A
Published by:
Design Community College, Inc
2016
eBook 51 pages
ISBN-10: 1-940805-16-3
ISBN-13: 978-1-940805-16-0

BRIEFING CHECK LISTS

PRODUCT DESIGN BRIEFING CHECKLIST

Author: Curedale, Robert A
Published by:
Design Community College, Inc.
Edition 1 2016
Paperback: 54 pages
Language: English
ISBN-10: 1940805317
ISBN-13: 978-1940805313

WEB DESIGN BRIEFING CHECKLIST

Author: Curedale, Robert A
Published by:
Design Community College, Inc.
Edition 1 November 2016
Paperback: 90 pages
Language: English
ISBN-10: 1940805287
ISBN-13: 978-1940805283

DESIGN THINKING PROCESS & METHODS GUIDE 2ND EDITION

Author: Curedale, Robert A
Published by:
Design Community College, Inc
January 2016
Paperback: 422 pages
Language: English
ISBN-10: 1-940805-20-1
ISBN-13: 978-1-940805-20-7

MAPPING METHODS

MAPPING METHODS 2
SET-BY-STEP GUIDE
EXPERIENCE MAPS
JOURNEY MAPS
SERVICE BLUEPRINTS
AFFINITY DIAGRAMS
EMPATHY MAPS

Author: Curedale, Robert
Published by:
Design Community College, Inc.
March 17 2018
Paperback: 312 pages
ISBN-10: 1940805376
ISBN-13: 978-1940805375

SERVICE BLUEPRINTS

2nd Edition
Author: Curedale, Robert
Published by:
Design Community College, Inc.
April 2019
Paperback
ISBN-10: 1940805406
ISBN-13: 978-1940805405

JOURNEY MAPS
STEP-BY-STEP GUIDE

2nd Edition
Author: Curedale, Robert
Design Community College, Inc
April 2019
Paperback 247 pages
ISBN-10: 1-940805-48-1
ISBN-13: 978-1-940805-48-1

EMPATHY MAPS
STEP-BY-STEP GUIDE

2nd Edition
Author: Curedale, Robert
Published by:
Design Community College, Inc
April 2019
Paperback
ISBN-10: 1-940805-47-3
ISBN-13: 978-1-940805-47-4

AFFINITY DIAGRAMS
STEP-BY-STEP GUIDE

2nd Edition
Author: Curedale, Robert
Published by:
Design Community College, Inc
April 2019
Paperback
ISBN-10: 1-940805-50-3
ISBN-13: 978-1-940805-50-4

CUSTOMER & USER
EXPERIENCE MAPS
STEP-BY-STEP GUIDE

2nd Edition
Author: Curedale, Robert A
Published by:
Design Community College, Inc.
February 2019
Paperback: 254 pages
Language: English
ISBN-10: 1-940805-46-5
ISBN-13: 978-1-940805-46-7

MAPPING METHODS

SERVICE BLUEPRINTS
First Edition
Author: Curedale, Robert
Published by:
Design Community College, Inc.
March 2016
Paperback: 152 pages
ISBN-10: 1940805198
ISBN-13: 978-1940805191

JOURNEY MAPS
First Edition
Author: Curedale, Robert
Published by:
Design Community College, Inc
March 2016
Paperback: 152 pages
Language: English
ISBN-10: 1940805228
ISBN-13: 978-1940805221

EMPATHY MAPS
First Edition
Author: Curedale, Robert
Published by:
Design Community College, Inc.
March 2016
Paperback: 152 pages
Language: English
ISBN-10: 1940805252
ISBN-13: 978-1940805252

AFFINITY DIAGRAMS
First Edition
Author: Curedale, Robert A
Published by:
Design Community College, Inc.
March 2016
Paperback: 128 pages
Language: English
ISBN-13 978-1940805269
ISBN-10 1940805269

MAPPING METHODS: FOR DESIGN AND STRATEGY
First Edition
Author: Curedale, Robert A
Published by:
Design Community College, Inc.
April 2013
Paperback: 136 pages
Language: English
ISBN-13 978-1940805269
ISBN-10 1940805269

SERVICE DESIGN

SERVICE DESIGN PROCESS & METHODS 3RD EDITION
Author: Curedale, Robert
Published by:
Design Community College, Inc
2018
Paperback: 532 pages
ISBN-10: 1940805368
ISBN-13: 978-1940805368

SERVICE DESIGN PROCESS & METHODS 2ND EDITION
Author: Curedale, Robert A
Published by:
Design Community College, Inc.
Edition May 2016
Paperback: 589 pages
Language: English
ISBN-10: 1-940805-30-9
ISBN-13: 978-1-940805-30-6

SERVICE DESIGN 250 ESSENTIAL METHODS
Author: Curedale, Robert A
Published by:
Design Community College, Inc.
Edition 1 Aug 01 2013
Paperback: 372 pages
Language: English
ISBN-10:0989246868
ISBN-13: 9780989246866

SERVICE DESIGN POCKET GUIDE
Author: Curedale, Robert A
Published by:
Design Community College, Inc.
Edition 1 Sept 01 2013
Paperback: 206 pages
Language: English
ISBN-10:0989246884
ISBN-13: 9780989246880

COLOR

DESIGNING WITH COLOR STEP-BY-STEP GUIDE
Author: Curedale, Robert A
Published by:
Design Community College, Inc.
Edition 1 July 01 2018
Paperback: 224 pages
Language: English
ISBN-10:1940805384
ISBN-13: 978-1940805382

DESIGN METHODS

DESIGN METHODS 1
200 WAYS TO APPLY
DESIGN THINKING

Author: Robert A Curedale
Published by:
Design Community College Inc.
Edition 1 November 2013
Paperback: 396 pages
Language: English
ISBN-10:0988236206
ISBN-13:978-0-9882362-0-2

DESIGN METHODS 2
200 MORE WAYS TO
APPLY DESIGN THINKING

Author: Robert A Curedale
Published by:
Design Community College Inc.
Edition 1 January 2013
Paperback: 398 pages
Language: English
ISBN-13: 978-0988236240
ISBN-10: 0988236249

50 SELECTED DESIGN METHODS

Author: Curedale, Robert A
Published by:
Design Community College, Inc.
Edition 1 Jan 17 2013
Paperback: 114 pages
Language: English
ISBN-10:0988236265
ISBN-13: 9780988236264

DESIGN RESEARCH

DESIGN RESEARCH
METHODS
150 WAYS TO
INFORM DESIGN

Author: Curedale, Robert A
Published by:
Design Community College, Inc.
Edition 1 January 2013
Paperback: 290 pages
Language: English
ISBN-10: 0988236257
ISBN-13: 978-0-988-2362-5-7

INTERVIEWS
OBSERVATION AND
FOCUS GROUPS

Author: Curedale, Robert A
Published by:
Design Community College, Inc.
Edition 1 Apr 01 2013
Paperback: 188 pages
Language: English
ISBN-10:0989246833
ISBN-13: 9780989246835

INTERVIEWS
OBSERVATION AND
FOCUS GROUPS

Author: Curedale, Robert A
Published by:
Design Community College, Inc.
Edition 1 Apr 01 2013
Paperback: 188 pages
Language: English
ISBN-10:0989246833
ISBN-13: 9780989246835

DESIGN RESEARCH

30 GOOD WAYS TO INNOVATE
Author: Curedale, Robert A
Design Community College, Inc.
Edition 1 November 2015
Paperback: 108 pages
Language: English
ISBN-10: 1940805139
ISBN-13: 978-1940805139

INTERVIEWS OBSERVATION AND FOCUS GROUPS
Author: Curedale, Robert A
Published by:
Design Community College, Inc.
Edition 1 Apr 01 2013
Paperback: 188 pages
Language: English
ISBN-10:0989246833
ISBN-13: 9780989246835

INTERVIEWS OBSERVATION AND FOCUS GROUPS
Author: Curedale, Robert A
Published by:
Design Community College, Inc.
Edition 1 Apr 01 2013
Paperback: 188 pages
Language: English
ISBN-10:0989246833
ISBN-13: 9780989246835

BRAINSTORMING

50 BRAINSTORMING METHODS
Author: Curedale, Robert A
Design Community College, Inc.
Edition 1 November 2015
Paperback: 108 pages
Language: English
ISBN-10: 1940805139
ISBN-13: 978-1940805139

DESIGN FOR CHINA

CHINA DESIGN INDEX THE ESSENTIAL DIRECTORY OF CONTACTS FOR DESIGNERS 2014
Author: Curedale, Robert A
Design Community College, Inc.
Edition 1 2014
Paperback: 384 pages
Language: English
ISBN-13: 978-1940805092
ISBN-101940805090

ABOUT THE AUTHOR

Rob Curedale was born in Australia and worked as a designer, director and educator in leading design offices in London, Sydney, Switzerland, Portugal, Los Angeles, Silicon Valley, Detroit, and Hong Kong. He designed or managed the design of over 1,000 products as a consultant and in-house design leader for the world's most respected brands. Rob has three decades experience in every aspect of product development and design research, leading design teams to achieve transformational improvements in operating and financial results. Rob's design scan be found in millions of homes and workplaces around the world and have generated billions of dollars in corporate revenues.

DESIGN PRACTICE
HP, Philips, GEC, Nokia, Sun, Apple, Canon, Motorola, Nissan, Audi VW, Disney, RTKL, Governments of the UAE,UK, Australia, Steelcase, Hon, Castelli, Hamilton Medical, Zyliss, Belkin, Gensler, Haworth, Honeywell, NEC, Hoover, Packard Bell, Dell, Black & Decker, Coleman and Harmon Kardon. Categories including furniture, healthcare, consumer electronics, sporting, housewares, military, exhibits, and packaging.

TEACHING
Rob has taught as a full time professor, adjunct professor and visiting instructor at institutions including the following: Art Center Pasadena, Art Center Europe, Yale School of Architecture, Pepperdine University, Loyola University, Cranbrook Academy of Art, Pratt, Otis, a faculty member at SCA and UTS Sydney, Chair of Product Design and Furniture Design at the College for Creative Studies in Detroit, then the largest product design school in North America, Cal State San Jose, Escola De Artes e Design in Oporto Portugal, Instituto De Artes Visuals, Design e Marketing, Lisbon, Southern Yangtze University, Jiao Tong University in Shanghai and Nanjing Arts Institute in China.

AWARDS
Designs that Rob has managed and designed have been recognized with IDSA IDEA Awards, Good Design Awards UK, Australian Design Awards, and a number of best of show innovation Awards at CES Consumer Electronics Show. His designs are in the Permanent collection of the Powerhouse Design Museum. In 2013 Rob was nominated for the Advanced Australia Award. The Awards celebrate Australians living internationally who exhibit "remarkable talent, exceptional vision, and ambition." In 2015 Rob was selected with a group of leading international industrial designers to provide opening comments for the International Congress Of Societies Of Industrial Design Conference ICSID in Korea.

www.ingramcontent.com/pod-product-compliance
Lightning Source LLC
Chambersburg PA
CBHW050553160426
43199CB00015B/2647